W.I.N.

N. K. Yama

Table of Contents

Mention of specific companies, organizations, individuals or authorities in this book does not imply endorsement by the author or publisher, nor does mention of specific companies, organizations, individuals or authorities imply that they endorse this book, its author or the publisher.

Dedication

This book is dedicated to the best support and love a man could ever hope for. Thank you for always inspiring, encouraging, and supporting me.

To my smoking hot wife, Lacey, who inspires me to pursue my dreams and follow my passions. She lifts, pushes, and pulls me to be the best version of myself.

My Children:

Izzy: My firstborn, who teaches me how to love and serve something or someone more than myself. The power of quiet determination and dedication.

Cooper: Who teaches me the value of unconditional love, respect, and service. He leads by humble dedication and example, and he refuses to be outworked.

Reese: Who teaches me to come out of my comfort zone and experience new things, to be the brightest light in the room.

Oxley: Who teaches me the value of humor, hard work, service and a good firm handshake.

Tillman: Who teaches me to believe in myself and chase my dreams no matter how high or how hard. That anything is possible.

Grit: Who teaches me how to stop and enjoy the moment, to live life, and to be in touch with my soul.

Dad & Grandfather: Who taught me the value of an honest, hard day's work and to keep working.

Mom: Who taught me selfless love and support. To see the good in everyone and every situation. To believe and trust in a higher power and plan. To serve a higher purpose.

Coaches: Who taught me the power of having someone believe in you and want the best success for you. Who held me to my highest potential and pushed me to exceed it.

Friends and Teammates: Who teach me the value of friendship, inspiration, support, and love.

God: Who continues providing me opportunities to grow, learn, listen, and love. He has blessed me beyond measure, and in His name, I dedicate this book.

Acknowledgement

Thank you first and foremost to my family for their unwavering support. I would be ungrateful if I did not acknowledge the mentors, leaders, teachers and coaches I have been blessed to have in my life; There are too many to name individually but have all made a lasting impression on who I am today.

To my teammates and peers, thank you for the hard lessons and for sharing in the victories, and failures. Thank you for the joys and the memories, thank you for teaching me humility, and giving me confidence. Thank you for your examples and thank you for your friendship.

To the athletes and clients, I have been privileged enough to coach, I have learned more from you than you have from me. It has truly been my honor and privilege to work with you, learn from you and be inspired by you. Always chase your commitments, control your controllables and be mindful of your perceptions. Remember that we are not our worst moment we are the victor that overcomes that moment and presses on.

The greatest compliment to receive is when others teach what you are teaching, when your ideas, beliefs, principles, and programs inspire others to improve themselves. By teaching a man to fish, he can feed his family, teach a man to teach others to fish and you can change the world. I have been inspired by so many outstanding men and women who are experts in their fields over the years that would be impossible to name them all. W.I.N. is a collection of inspiration, teaching, principles, ideals, habits, beliefs and programs that I have accepted, adapted, and integrated into my own life, coaching and program.

Finally, thank you for allowing me an opportunity to come into your home, business, school and be part of your team. To share my passion for sports, business, family, improvement and success. I hope this book and its philosophies, ideas and practices help you along your journey to your own success and high performance in all the little and big things you do. Take what works for you, add it into your life and make it yours. It is my pleasure to introduce you to W.I.N.

"Winning is not a sometime thing; it's an all-time thing. You don't win once in a while, you don't do things right once in a while, you do them right all the time. Winning is habit. Unfortunately, so is losing." -Vince Lombardi

Introduction

The principles, practices, and lessons introduced in this book are based on years of personal and professional experience as a player, mentor, and coach. It is the culmination of over 30 years of sports, business, family, fatherhood, marriage, success, failure, and effort. I have found sports to be the great similitude of life. Every season is like its own little lifetime with new goals, challenges, players, and competition. Every year presents new opportunities, and if you aren't willing to change and adapt, you start to fall behind. When things start to go bad, it is easy to see the negativity spread quickly and how it affects the team, each player, coach, school, and even the community.

The W.I.N. program is not complex, it is not difficult to understand—it is the sacrifice required that is hard. Everyone wants to win until it comes time do what it required to win. I believe in focusing on the process (the journey) not the result, creating habits of effort, attitude, and character. Outstanding habits lead to outstanding character which leads to outstanding results. By only focusing on the outcome or desired result, score, medal, ring, or trophy, you are limiting yourself and the heights of success you are allowing yourself to achieve. Do not allow yourself to be caught up in competition (victory, defeat, being better than another, or chasing a singular result). Focus on the process, create habits, develop a strong character, and you will experience levels of success you didn't think were possible. The greatest predictor of success in sports (and life) is the mental preparation, fortitude, and resolve of the participants involved.

Winning is NOT being superior to another person, or team, that is the competition. Ted lasso said it best: *"I believe you can outscore your opponent and still lose, just like you can score less than them and win."* Oxford Languages defines winning as: *be successful or victorious in (a contest or conflict).* Coach John Wooden defined success as *"peace of mind attained only through self-satisfaction in knowing you made the effort to do the best of which you're capable."* If winning is to be successful, Coach Wooden perfectly defines what it is to win. Don't strive to be superior or better than someone else, strive to be better than your previous self. Being successful and being victorious are not defined by a score, a trophy, ring or medal. It is defined by the attitude, effort, development, and character of the participant.

If you need someone to compete with, compete with yourself; if you need someone to chase, chase your best self; if you need someone to beat, beat your previous self. You can't make a shot you don't take; you can't hit a home run if you don't swing, and you can't win if you aren't willing to try.

How to use this book

There is no perfect blueprint to winning, if there was, there would be a lot more successful people. The world is full of examples of people that did things in totally opposite ways, went against conventional wisdom, or the experts all said would fail that have achieved immense success. There is not a blueprint model that anyone can follow that will lead to success; there are, however, common practices, traits, skills and patterns that the ultra-successful all have and use. WIN identifies those elements; outlines how and why they work and teaches you how to incorporate them into your own life. The true secret to success is to find what works and what doesn't. The goal and purpose of WIN is to create a process and program that works for you individually.

W.I.N. is designed to help guide you through the creation, implementation, and practice of your own WIN system. It is NOT a checklist or a to do manual. I can't do it for you; no one can! So stop trying to copy others. Stop looking for the right program, the right book, the right coach, or the right way and focus on <u>your</u> way. This book can be a great resource for you as you create your own system and practices, but like everything else in the world, it only works if you do!

W.I.N. will engage your mind and your emotions, it will help you see things in a different perception, and it will open you up to possibilities and ideas. When you are finished, you will have your own personal direction, and road map to becoming a WINner.

You will find activities throughout the book. I highly recommend that you stop reading and complete each activity before you continue, especially the first time. If you are using this as a workbook for your team, staff, office or group, you may find it beneficial to do the activities individually and collectively.

This book is designed to be used as a reference/training manual. As you advance in skill, age and accomplishment your commitments, your goals, and your focus will change; it is important to review and update your goals/commitments regularly. The principles, practices and activities in this book apply to teams as well as individuals. It is just as important to set team, group, company, and committee goals and commitments as it is to your individual success. I encourage you to use this program as an annual training activity with your team, family, and as an individual.

You are like an ATM machine; the more you put into yourself, the more you can withdraw. The same is true with anything you do; you get out what you put in.

Coaches and Teams: The principles and practices of W.I.N. are beneficial to both individuals and teams alike. Refer to the "TEAM" Section on all activities to apply the activity to your team, group or family. Have each individual participate in the activity on a personal level as well as the team activity.

Chapter 1 – Core Principles

W.I.N. is built on a foundation of 3 core principles, truths, and beliefs that are essential for your growth and success. To reach your full potential, growth is necessary, and these principles directly shape your ability to learn and improve. Think back to when you learned to walk. You probably don't remember, but you stumbled countless times, but you kept trying, learning, and progressing. You believed walking was possible because everyone around you could do it. You didn't compare yourself to others; instead, you were encouraged by family to keep going at your own pace, without pressure or anxiety. You didn't feel discouraged by each fall; you simply got back up, determined to try again until you mastered not only walking but eventually running, jumping, and even skipping. This mindset applies to all pursuits: don't fear failure. Keep striving, keep moving forward, and you will ultimately surpass your own expectations.

1: Be Perceptional.

"Perception is reality, but it may not be actuality, and you have got to be able to keep the difference between that."– Bill Cowher

Your perceptions create the foundation for your mental, emotional, and physical responses to challenges, success, and interaction. Being Perceptional is the ability to acknowledge that every situation, comment, act, or event has multiple different perceptions and recognize that there are multiple choices, options, and opportunities. It is about taking in all the sensory information and recognizing how your personal beliefs affect your current feelings and opinions on a certain topic, situation, event, or person(s).

Your perceptions shape the way you view the world. They are the lenses through which you interpret events, people, comments, situations, etc. Influencing your thoughts, decisions, relationships, values, self-worth, motivations, actions, reactions and so on. Often, your perspectives become fixed, limiting your ability to understand and empathize with others who hold different viewpoints or accept other possibilities than you. When this happens, you naturally find excuses, become less and less accountable, coachable, and responsible. You perceive yourself as not in control, and that becomes your reality. Your perceptions are the walls that you surround yourself with; they create your comfort zone. Your comfort zone is your prison, not allowing anything in or out. Growth and success are achieved by breaking through those walls and tearing them down.

Your perceptions frame your reality, and everyone's perceptions are unique, also meaning that everyone's reality is unique. Acknowledging and accepting that there are multiple perceptions to everything, and everyone is the key to unlocking your full potential. Excuses, negativity, frustration, defensiveness and justification are all byproducts of your perceptions. Do not allow your perceptions to imprison you from being coachable, from learning, growing trying new things, and experiencing new perceptions.

Your perceptions are manifest in your attitude; those two things together create your ego. Your attitude is more important than your ability or talent. You can learn the process and be taught the skills; however, a negative, entitled, defeatist, or victim attitude is the number one thing that will destroy your ability to succeed. A negative attitude leads to quitting, blaming others, excuses and ultimately failure. The desire to perform, the appreciation of the opportunity and the love of the moment are all part of a positive attitude; that attitude is the engine to committed effort and success. Different perceptions and attitudes lead to different results. Positive perceptions and attitude will create a positive ego and reap positive results. Negative perceptions and attitude will do the opposite.

Be positive, be coachable, be accountable, be responsible and be Perceptional.

2: Always do your best!

"It's not about what you're capable of, It's about what you're willing to do." -Mike Tomlin

Fear of failure, fear of ridicule and being laughed at, fear of comparison, fear of rejection, fear of unworthiness, and even fear of success can be paralyzing. You want to be perfect before you start. The good news is that there is a simple way to overcome those fears... Do YOUR Best! Don't try and do or outdo someone else's best; be your best right now, in this moment, in everything you do.

Your number one fear is that you are not good enough; it doesn't matter what the context is—friendships, relationships, profession, sports, education, hobbies, talents, goals, dreams—it all comes back to the one basic fear of not being good enough.

If you are always competing and comparing yourself to others, you will always exist with some level of fear. Always doing your best is the ONLY way to effectively remove the fears and pressures you place on yourself.

Your best today should be better than your best yesterday but not as good as your best tomorrow. Improve daily; 1% improvement every day is 365% over a year! Your greatness takes time, effort, patience and resilience. Always do your best, in every way, every day!

There is a popular saying: "How you do anything is how you do everything." I want to take it a step further. The effort and care you put into anything you do effects everything you do. If you dress sloppy, always show up late, have bad hygiene, make excuses, blame others, complete tasks at the last minute, etc., you are setting a standard in your life for how you will do everything. How you do everything, even the seemingly mundane and small tasks, is training yourself how to perform in anything you do—big or small, important or routine—it all matters. You are setting a minimum acceptable standard in your life, and it takes concentrated effort to do more than the minimum required amount to complete a task. Raise your minimum standard, take the time, make the effort, give your best in ALL things you do.

Engaging in even the small tasks with care, attention, and consistency will naturally carry over into the bigger, more important tasks and challenges. On the other hand, if you tend to cut corners and let the little things slide, those habits will also carry forward. The way you approach anything, no matter how trivial, sets the tone for everything you do.

It's not just about doing things well; it's about developing a mindset of excellence in all that you do.

On a team, everyone's contributions matter, and by holding yourself and your teammates the highest standard in everything you do will develop the discipline and resilience needed to tackle bigger challenges and inspire others to do the same.

It's all connected, and by always striving to do your best in everything you do, you are setting yourself up for greater success and performance.

There is a great quote that some attribute to St. Jerome and others to Tim Duncan either way it carries a very powerful message. "Good, better, best. Never let it rest. Until your good is better and your better is best." Good is the enemy of best. So often we allow ourselves to settle for "good enough" or "that's good." Don't allow yourself, your team, your peers, family or friends to fall into this trap. Do your best. The more you do your best, the better your best becomes. You will never know your full potential unless you continually do your best, all the time, in everything you do.

3: Life is a journey, not an event.

"It's all about the journey, not the outcome." – Carl Lewis

You are not defined by one event, one play, one win, or one loss, but rather by the sum of your experiences, choices, and actions. It is the accumulation of moments, both significant and seemingly mundane, that shape your character, values, and identity. Your resilience in the face of adversity, your capacity for empathy and compassion, and your commitment to growth and self-improvement are what truly define you.

In 2009, Tiger Woods' personal life became the subject of intense public scrutiny and a highly publicized scandal. Woods' reputation as a role model was tarnished, as he faced widespread criticism and condemnation from both the media and the public. Woods took a break from golf to focus on personal issues, rebuilding his reputation, and repairing his relationships with his family and loved ones.

In 2019, Tiger Woods achieved one of the greatest comebacks in sports history when he won the Masters Tournament. His triumph was a testament to his resilience, perseverance, and ability to overcome adversity. Woods' journey from personal crisis to redemption serves as a powerful example of the human capacity for growth, forgiveness, and second chances. His story inspires millions of people around the world to confront their own challenges with courage and determination, knowing that it is possible to rise above adversity and achieve greatness once again.

There is not one event that defines you unless you let it. You will have more chances, you will have more opportunities. Life is a journey, and the journey defines who you are, not an event or outcome. The secret to success, to overcoming obstacles, to growth and improvement, to getting through heartache, embarrassment and trials is all the same.

KEEP WORKING!

During an actor's roundtable, Tom Hanks said, *"You feel bad right now, you feel pissed off...this too shall pass. You feel angry...this too shall pass. You feel great, you feel like you know all the answers, you feel like everybody finally gets you...this too shall pass. Time is your ally, and if nothing else…just wait, just wait…just wait it out."* What a great testament to the journey of life. Life keeps moving, the world keeps moving, you need to keep moving with it. The only way to truly and completely fail is to quit. Life is a journey, not a singular event. Do not allow yourself to be defined by one singular moment, even if that moment was an amazing accomplishment. Do not settle, do not quit, do not be satisfied! EVER!

WIN.

"To win, you have to lose. To be successful, you got to have something that's not successful. To be happy, you have to have disappointment. All of those things have evolved & happened to make me who I am." - Michael Jordan

You will struggle, you will stumble, and you will fall. The world is a nasty cutthroat place; the more success you achieve the harder it becomes. People are jealous, they are vindictive, and they are mean; you will be attacked, you will be slandered, and you will be ridiculed. You will come face to face with your biggest fears. You will encounter loss, defeat, and rejection. You will want to quit, give up, and question if it is worth it. You will be tested, tried, pushed and pulled, you will sweat, you will cry, and you will bleed, *"Winning will cost you everything, and reward you with more, if you're willing to do the work." -Tim Grover (Winning: The Unforgiving Race to Greatness)*

These core values are the foundation to WIN, and by cultivating them in your life, in everything you do, you are building your foundation to winning and success. Your toughest opponent is your fear, your biggest enemy is your ego (perceptions), your strongest competition is yourself, and your greatness has yet to be realized.

If you are ready to discover what it means to you to win, if you are willing to pay the price required to achieve winning, then I am excited to take the journey with you.

Chapter 2 – W (The Fundamentals)

"Success is neither magical nor mysterious. Success is the natural consequence of consistently applying the basic fundamentals." - Jim Rohn

Success in sports and life come down to one thing: how well you know and execute the fundamentals. There are always fancy new fads, new training techniques, trick plays, fast tracks, short cuts, and so on, but winning and success is achieved and sustained through fundamentals.

Hall of Fame Coach Bill Parcells was notorious for emphasizing and focusing on the fundamentals with his teams. "Even to my veteran players, I never was afraid to implement the most elementary fundamentals: the stance, the take-off, the fire-out, the defensive charge, the linebacker-block protection, the defensive backs' technique as far as mid points of zones, man-to-man, press and off coverage. Lots of things, fundamentally, must be stressed. I didn't take for granted that even the veteran players were up to speed. Now, most of the time they were, but by not being afraid to repeat those fundamentals, I think that that kind of solidified the things in the player's mind that I thought were important." If he emphasized these simple basic football fundamentals with his professional, Super Bowl champion and hall of fame players, you know how important those fundamentals were to him and to winning.

Your W's: Who, what, where, when and why are your fundamentals. They are your goals, commitments, motivations, dedications, and reasons for doing what you do and making you who you are. Your fundamentals define you; they are the reason why you are who you are and why you do what you do. They are the foundation of your character, your purpose, your goals and dreams and your personal definition of winning.

Character is defined by Oxford Languages as "the mental and moral qualities distinctive to an individual." Your character is the culmination of your mental and moral traits. Honesty, discipline, effort, trustworthy, loyal, dedication, these are just a few of the character traits essential for success. Coach Vince Lombardi added, *"Character is just another word for having a perfectly disciplined and educated will. A person can make his own character by blending these elements with an intense desire to achieve excellence. Everyone is different in what I will call magnitude, but the capacity to achieve character is still the same.*" Character is about one thing: YOUR PERSONAL BEST! Always be your best, always do your best, and always strive for your best.

It is simple to create a list of wants (most people call them goals). It is simple to put a schedule and plan together that will lead you to accomplishing those wants/goals. On paper, it is easy to accomplish those wants. If I do this, this, and this, then I will accomplish my goal. Unfortunately, it is not that easy. There are always outside influences, challenges, hardships, and setbacks. There is no checklist to achieving success, and there is no shortcut.

The question is does your character to match your desire. Are your wants (goals) in alignment with who you are and who you want to become?

Defining your W's (fundamentals) is defining your wants (goals) and aligning those with your character. When they are alignment you will win, in fact, you can't lose; but when they aren't, you will fight an uphill battle against your toughest opponent (yourself) and you will fail more than you will win. Your W's are the roadmap to win. They are your commitments, expectations, and ultimately the results. To know what it takes to win, you need to know where you're starting from, where you want to go, and how you are going to get there. Your W's do just that!

"The minute you get away from fundamentals—whether its proper technique, work ethic or mental preparation—the bottom can fall out of your game, your schoolwork, your job, whatever you're doing."
-Michael Jordan

WHO

"Who you are is more important than what you do, how high you jump, how fast you run, because who you are is your character. Your character is an accumulation of your thoughts, your habits, and your priorities on a day-to-day basis. Those three things determine the choices you make and the choices you make, make you who you are. Good guy, bad guy, hardworking, lazy, responsible, irresponsible, and it takes a certain amount of discipline to do what you're supposed to do, when you're supposed to do it, the way it's supposed to get done." -Nick Saban

There are three people you need to know to achieve success in life. Who you are now, who you want to become, and God. Knowing who you are influences your emotions, attitude, actions, motivation, dedication, and more. Knowing who you want to become is your ultimate purpose, it is your long-term goal; it sets a standard for your decisions and actions. By knowing who you are and who you want to become, you are defining your success. You are establishing your starting point and your destination. By knowing God, you are enlisting a higher power in pursuit of that destination (goal). God knows you, God loves you, and God wants you to be happy. Knowing God and making him a part of who you are is allowing God's will and success into your life. You are never alone; with God all things are possible. Belief in a higher power (God) is a very powerful force of inspiration, dedication, love, commitment and purpose. Those are all key elements of a winner.

Q: Who are you?

"You are who you are when nobody's watching." - Stephen Fry.

Tell me what you think about when you don't have to think, and I will tell you how successful you will be. It is easy to follow the crowd, to go with the flow, it is much more difficult to stay true to your personal beliefs and commitments when no one is around, when no one will know but you. These are your personal core values.

Activity 1:

Write down 10 positive things about yourself. (Example: hard working, good at math, generous, motivated, love baseball, dedicated, a brother, daughter, mother, good teammate, honest, dependable, motivated, etc.) Once you have your list, pick your top three (make sure they are focused on different traits or qualities, avoid having all three centered around the same thing) Write the words "I AM" in front of your top 3. Congratulations! You have just created the basis for your I am affirmation statement.

<u>Team:</u> Create a list of 10 core values as a team. These define your team culture, direction, and purpose.

Q: Who do you want to be?

This isn't just one name but rather a collection of traits that you want to become. I am sure you have multiple people in your life that you admire and aspire to be like in some way. The traits that you admire are important foundational pieces to who you want to be, and how you want to be remembered. They are not a profession, a hobby, or financial wealth, they are the core principles you personally stand for, and emulate. How do you want to be remembered? What is your legacy going to be?

Activity 2:

Write down 5 people you admire. Under their name, write the 1-3 traits that you admire and want to incorporate into your own life and why.

<u>Team:</u> Create a list of 5 teams your team admires and 1-3 traits or practices that you want to incorporate into your team culture, practice, or purpose. These can be on any level of competition.

Q: Who is God?

God looks and feels a little different to everyone. For some, God is a higher power more than a being. For others, God is a friend or a father, and for some, God is just an ideal or teaching. Your personal definition of God is not as important as your desire to know him and to serve Him. When God is a part of who you are, the goals you set, the commitments you make, and the actions you take; you are always on the right path to success. God is not an excuse for giving up, not having control, or not giving your best effort. Too often people use God as a crutch or an excuse for their current standing or result. You will have to work, you will stumble, you will learn and grow, but always remember: God is undefeated; if you want to W.I.N., He is a great teammate to have.

Activity 3:

Take a moment and write your own eulogy. Who is giving the address? And what do you want them to say about you? How do you want to be remembered? Who do you want to be remembered as? Write your eulogy in a bullet point format so that you can clearly identify the answers and traits. After reading back through it several times, rate on a scale of 1-5 (5 being the best) how you feel you are doing on each trait. You now have a score card to help you identify areas of strength and areas of focus and improvement.

- <u>*Team:*</u> *When the season is over, create a list of things your team wants to be remembered for as a team and individually. How do to the older members want to be remembered by their teammates, community, coaches etc.*

Q: Who is responsible/accountable?

The answer to this question is always you! You are always responsible for your emotions, actions, reactions, thoughts, effort, and attitude. You cannot directly control another's action or decisions; however, you absolutely have power and influence over you, how you respond, think, speak, and act. Being accountable for the role you play in any and every situation is a huge step toward realizing success. Can you control how much a coach plays you? Maybe not directly, but you can control the effort you put in on and off the court, during and away from practice. You can control your attitude toward teammates, coaches, challenges, and opportunities. You can control your ability to improve and perform to your peak performance. Be accountable for you, be responsible for you. Did you give your very best the all the time? (Not just during the season but all year? In class? At home?) You can only improve if you are accountable to yourself and acknowledge that improvements need to be made to achieve success. Why would you change anything if nothing is your fault? Excuses are poison, they slowly kill you from the inside, they destroy effort, they erode accountability, and they give power to others while removing yours. *"Average players want to be left alone. Good players want to be coached. Great players want to be told the truth." - Doc Rivers.* Ask yourself, do you want to be average, good, or great? Be responsible, be accountable, be coachable, and you will be successful.

Activity 4:

- *Write down 10 things that you are responsible and accountable for (e.g., attitude, effort, actions and reactions etc.).*
- <u>*Team:*</u> *As a team what are the top 10 things you have control over on and*

off the field. What are 10 things you are accountable for as a team (e.g., to your teammates, coaches, community, etc.)?

Q: Who is in control?

The answer to this question at any time should be YOU, however often we give this control to other people or to our own emotional responses (e.g., anger, excitement, jealousy, pride, ego, etc.). If you're not in control to make the adjustments necessary to reach your goal(s), then who will do it for you? You are in control and by being in control there is no fear, no nervousness, no pressure, just opportunity.

"Watch your actions, they become your habits. Watch your habits, they become your character." -Vince Lombardi

Activity 5:

- *Write down 10 things that you are absolutely in control of.*
- *Write down 10 things that you want control of in your life.*
- *(Examples: being on time, work ethic, attitude, etc.)*
- *<u>Team:</u> Write down 10 things you are in control of as a team? And 10 things you want to have more control over, now and through the season.*

WIN:

Who you are and who you want to become set the starting point and destination against which your progress and success is measured. Identifying, stating, and repeating who you are is a powerful tool for focus, discipline and decision making.

1: Who is responsible?

2: Who is in control?

3: Who are you?(This is your I am statement from activity 1)

Repeat the answers to these three questions often throughout your day. Make these statements part of your daily routine. Start and end your day with these three questions. During times of challenge, struggle, stress, anxiety or other situations of high emotion, taking a deep breath and asking yourself these three simple questions will immediately calm your emotions, focus your thinking, and redirect your energy into a positive response, effort, and result. There are always hills to climb and bumps in the road, but there is always a way if you know who you are, who is responsible, and who is in control then success is within your reach!

WHAT / WANT

Now that you have defined who you are, it is time to establish what you want. Your "What" is your wants, desires and goal(s).

"The only real limitation is the one you set for yourself."
- Muhammad Ali

Q: What do you want?

This is the hardest easy question in the world. It is easy to start rambling off a list of what you think you want, but as you will discover later, what you think you want vs. the effort, time, and sacrifice it will take to get it doesn't always match.

Let's talk about goals. There are literally hundreds if not thousands of books on goals, how to set them, tricks to accomplishing them, etc. Goals are possibly the most talked about, most engaged in, most emphasized, most misunderstood, and biggest waste of time in the world of sports, business, life coaching, self-improvement, etc. Every year millions of people set New Year's resolutions, and according to studies conducted over the last 10 years, only about 18% of those goals are stuck with after one year. Those aren't very impressive numbers for success. Goals without action, intention, effort and a plan for success are just a wish!

I use the word commitment rather than goal. A commitment is a goal with a promise of action, not just a stated hopeful objective. *(Oxford languages defines commitment as: the state or quality of being dedicated to a cause, activity, etc.)* When you are committed to something, someone or some purpose you are willing to give everything within your ability to see that commitment through. Commitment is also lasting, goals are achieved (or not) and then forgotten, you set another goal and another goal and while this process can be effective for some, it hasn't proven to be effective for the masses. When you are committed to something, that doesn't go away, that doesn't end; even after achieving whatever you were committed to do, you retain your commitment to that skill, attribute, person, etc.

When you are committed to a team, the team comes first. When you are committed to a caue or purpose , the accomplishment of that purpose becomes a priority over anything that is in the way of that commitment. When you are committed to a person, you are loyal, trustworthy and fight for their best interests, success and happiness just like your own. <u>Do NOT set goals. Set commitments!</u>

Q: What am I willing to do or sacrifice to get what I want?

This answer to this question will tell you how likely you are to achieve success. To be great at something, you will need to be willing to sacrifice being great at something else. We are all given the same amount of time in every day, week, month, and year. To be great, there is a cost that must be paid. That payment of your time, efforts, relationships, thoughts and is due daily. Knowing what you want is the only way to W.I.N. If you find yourself lacking motivation, struggling with reaching milestones, not improving and lacking interest, not growing toward your goals, then you are chasing someone else's wants. Competition, challenges, trials and struggles will show you what you really want. When things get tough your true desires (wants) become clear. When you are in pursuit of your wants, there is no shortage of motivation, no lack of focus or interest. You will run, walk, crawl and scrape your way through hell to reach your end goal. You will be committed.

Your "what" is the thing that every decision should be weighed against and in alignment with. For example if your "what" is to earn a starting spot on the varsity team (or a promotion at work) and you have been invited to go out with your friends to a party, but that means you will miss practice, the decision should not be based of the momentary or instant gratification that the party will provide; but because you know your "what," you are able to make a decision that moves you closer to accomplishing that commitment.

Keep in mind that the purpose of setting and achieving goals and commitments is not to make the varsity team, get the scholarship, achieve the promotion, make the money, etc. The real reward is the person you become in the process—who you are, what you have learned, who you have met and touched along the way and the new skills you have developed, are the true definition of success. Some people reach goals by lying, cheating, stealing, or just pure luck, but their success is empty and lonely. The strongest "whats" are not material things, but rather they are skills, relationships, experiences, love and service. It is not wrong to want to be the star, but it is even better to want to be the one who gives back and helps others, and if the best way to do that is through your success, then that is a great what to want!

Activity 7:

- *List your wants, make a new column for each category (personal, professional, spiritual, emotional, etc.) List your "wants" under the appropriate category (3-5 wants per category).*
- *Next to each "want," add a number 1-5, 5 being the highest priority (you are only allowed one 5 per column.)*
- *Review this list tomorrow and again in a week and make any adjustments to your ratings.*
- *Once you have identified your top wants for each category write them on the top of their own column (2 per page max) These are your goals / commitments.*
- *<u>Team:</u> As a team list your wants following the same categories as the individual activity. It is important set, discuss, and pursue goals in each category as a team, it allows leaders to get to know teammates, and coaches to see what is important to their team on a personal level.*

WIN:

Success is not about what you want, what you can do, or what you know, it is about what you are willing to do to achieve it. Identify your want(s), create your commitments, and then don't stop until you WIN.

WHERE

"You can't know where you're going until you know where you've been." -Maya Angelou

Your "where" is your reality. As discussed previously, it is vitally important to be perceptional with yourself, your situation, and your surroundings. Where is not a physical location or destination but a figurative one. One element that is not often discussed when people talk about setting, and achieving commitments, is the where—where you are starting from, where you are now, and where you want to end up.

How often do you find yourself thinking about other things when you are in the middle of a task or activity? How often does your mind wander? Are you disinterested in many of your daily tasks and activities? Identifying your "where" is knowing the starting place on the map. Once you know where you are starting from, you can find the best route to get to your desired destination.

Q: Where did you start?

As mentioned above, it is essential to your success to know where you are starting from, picture life as a journey and when you know where you are starting from and you know where you are going or wanting to go, you know where you are along the journey. You know how far you have come; you know how far you need to go.

Q: Where do you fit?

Where do you fit (what is your role) in your family? At work? Amongst your peers? On your team? What is your role? How does your exception performance in that role propel you toward where you want to end up?

Q: Where are you now?

Where on your journey to achieving success and accomplishing your commitments are you? Where amongst your peers are you? Are you on the right path to where you want to be? You might be working hard and moving forward, but if it's not in the direction of where you want to end up, you are wasting time and energy.

?Q: Where do you want to end up

Your commitments are your destinations. These destinations are anything you set as a commitment (goal), they can be a position on the team or at work, a promotion, a weight or fitness goal, etc. When you can clearly identify where you want to end up, it is much easier to set destinations (milestones) along your journey to your ultimate destination.

Knowing where you started, where you are, and where you want to go allows you to identify the wants that are not on the same path, and either change your direction or remove those "off course" destinations. Creating a plan with your milestones in alignment with your destination is the fast track to success.

Activity 8:

- *Draw a ladder with 10 steps on the left side of a piece of paper.*
- *On the top of the ladder write down where you want to end up. Your goal/ commitment.*
- *On the bottom write 3-5 of your core values and beliefs that provide a strong foundation toward your end goal. (Staying true to these values will get you to the top of the ladder.)*
- *For each step, write down an achievement or landmark that needs to be achieved to keep climbing.*
- *Now cross off the steps that you have already climbed. If you are just starting, that is a great place to be starting from.*
- **This exercise can be used for short term, long term, and even lifetime commitments. Where along the ladder are you? How many more steps do you have to reach the top? Some ladders might be longer than 10 but no matter the end destination. There are always steps along the way. Identifying and staying true to the foundation that you set your ladder on is key to the stability of the ladder as you climb. When your foundation isn't solid the ladder will sway, and rock and ultimately can fall over. Make sure your ladder is on a strong foundation of core beliefs. If your end destination isn't in alignment with those values, you're a climbing a crooked ladder.*
- *<u>Team:</u> Create a team ladder! I recommend having the top of the ladder something that is accomplished over multiple years. Victories are great but if that is your ultimate goal, you will struggle with culture and sustained success year after year.*

You Never Know How Close You Are To Greatness:
"The difference between ordinary and extraordinary is that little extra." - Jimmy Johnson

Take out your ladder (from activity 8) Imagine if that was an actual ladder in front of you, and you know that if you make it to the top of the ladder, you will accomplish your goals, desires, and dreams, Would you stop climbing when you could see the top? Would you slow down as you got closer, or would you feel invigorated and push harder and faster? If you can see the top of the ladder, no matter how high, you will know how much effort you need to put in, you will be able to track your progress, and when you slip down a few steps, you will still know how far you have left to go. You will have twice as much motivation and adrenaline in your system to make up for the steps lost.

Some people would still not even start, and others would go so far and stop, but so many more would make it to the top just because they know where the top is. You can see progress every day. With every step, you get a little closer. You are treading in the right direction. On the days it is hard to climb, you know if I just move up one step today, I will have less to do tomorrow and the next day, etc. You never know how close to greatness you are. One more rep, one more practice, one more week, month, year, could be all it takes, and if you quit, you will never find out! Whether I fail or succeed, I know that my real victory lies in working, learning and grrowing That is the only way to succeed in life. You may not get there today, but you are getting closer to it, and you will get there. The key is to keep working. You're so close to Greatness.

WIN:
Conscious awareness of where you are along your journey to greatness Is a vital piece of the puzzle. Knowing where you are provides clarity and focus on your commitments and how close you are to achieving them.

WHEN

"When" is your action, your effort, and your intention. Your when is one of the biggest indicators of success. Are you willing to start now? Or do you need to plan, think, evaluate, and talk it over? Are you willing to go to work now, or do you need to make sure you are an expert first?

"A man would do nothing if he waited until he could do it so well that no one could find fault." - John Henry Newman

One of the hardest things to teach, coach, and understand is the concept of time. We all think we have more time, in reality, we never have enough. Unfortunetly, most of us don't learn this lesson until we have wasted a lot of it. The importance of time cannot be overstated, it is the one thing that we all have the same amount of and can't get more. How you choose to use it will determine your level of success.

Q: When will you start?

Now or do you need to wait until tomorrow, next week or after this vacation, weekend, or event? If you are wanting to start a diet, why do you need to wait until Monday? Or even tomorrow? Start right now! You can't finish if you don't start.. Get going and get going right now!

Q: When do you want to accomplish the task or goal?

Set guidelines, deadlines and ladders or steps. Set a long-term timeline and then breakdown your commitment into smaller, shorter deadlines. You can track progress; you can track results, and you will stay motivated with smaller successes along your journey.

Q: When will you make time?

"I just don't have time." - Everyone.

You say it, I say it, everyone says it. This is by far the number one excuse for lack of action, success, and commitment in the world. You are blaming something that we all have the same amount of, that we can all control, and that no matter the amount of money or talent you can't get more of. <u>You make time for the things that are important to you...period!</u> End of discussion! So, the real question you need to ask yourself is when will this be important enough to me to make time?

WIN:

Start NOW. Do it NOW. Now is the time. There is no better time to start anything than right now. Most of the world is great at coming up with goals and they are going to start them all tomorrow, or right after this vacation or event, or next week. Procrastination is just an excuse before you need to come up with one. If you never start or are "to busy" to start, then you can never fail. If you wait to be great at something before you try it, then you will never accomplish anything. Fear is your biggest enemy, it isn't athletic ability, mental acuity or even opportunity it is fear. Starting Now doesn't eliminate fear, but it doesn't allow it to grow and fester in your mind and even worse in your heart, it looks it right in the eye and says, "let's go."

Nothing in this world was ever accomplished without starting, so start NOW.

WHY

"You have to be burning with an idea, or a problem, or a wrong that you want to right. If you're not passionate enough from the start, you'll never stick it out." - Steve Jobs

You have identified what you want. Now it is time to figure out why you want what you want, and why you do what you do.

Q: What is your why?

"Regardless of whatever I do, I know what my purpose is: to make a difference in people's lives." -Tim Tebow.

Your why is your personal statement of purpose that describes why you do what you do! It is your reason for getting out of bed in the morning. It is your calling. It is your conviction. It is your mission statement. It is the reference point for all your decisions and actions to be based. If you are feeling overwhelmed, anxious, pressure, bored, unsatisfied or unfulfilled, you don't have a clear understanding of your why. Your "why" comes from within you.. Your why is what will drive you when the going gets tough. It's what gives your goals meaning and purpose. Knowing your why is the difference between merely wanting something and going out and getting something It is the combination of your values, passions, and purpose.

<u>Values:</u> *"Values are like fingerprints. Nobody's are the same, but you leave them all over everything you do." – Elvis Presley*

Values are the foundation for your why. They define what is important to you and influence the passions you pursue and the purpose you seek to fulfill. Your values are what make up your character, they are the traits you admire, desire and hold dear. They are the foundation of who you are. Your values shine through in times of trial, challenge and pressure. Identify the values you want, list the values you have, and then work to make those match. When you pass on from this life, your values are what remain. They are your legacy.

<u>Passion:</u> *"Nothing great in the world has ever been accomplished without passion."*-Georg Wilhelm Friedrich Hegel

Passion is the emotional attachment you have to a cause, task, idea, thought, person or desire. Passion is what drives you to explore and engage in activities aligned with your values. It is the strong and intense emotional drive that fuels your pursuit of your goals and commitments. Passion is the emotion that creates a high level of commitment and desire to keep working towards your goals, even when times are hard.

Purpose: *"There is no failure except failure to serve one's purpose." -Henry Ford*

Purpose is how and when your values and passions come together. It is a sense of meaning and direction in your life that goes beyond personal enjoyment or fulfillment. Purpose often involves contributing to the greater good or serving a cause larger than yourself. Your purpose is a collection of your talents, passions, desires, and inspirations. You have been blessed with an individual collection of talents and skills that make you special. Your purpose is your who, thecore values that make up your character. Your purpose is not a vague notion, but a clear and concrete objective that gives your life direction and meaning. Money is the result of your work, but it's your why (purpose) that fuels your work. If your purpose is to make a difference in people's lives, you can do that in anything you do, in any job, activity, role, title and responsibility.

"If it falls your lot to be a street sweeper, go out and sweep streets like Michelangelo painted pictures. Sweep streets like Handel and Beethoven composed music. Sweep streets like Shakespeare wrote poetry. Sweep streets so well that all the hosts of heaven and earth will have to pause and say, here lived a great street sweeper who swept his job well." – Martin Luther King, Jr.

The street sweeper made a difference in people's lives through taking pride in his work, always doing his best, and keeping his streets clean, reducing disease, rodents, and keeping the city looking its best. If money was his purpose, he probably would have hated his job, felt unfulfilled and underpaid. There is purpose in every task, every action and every interaction you have. Serving a higher purpose than yourself is one of the most powerful forces in your life. It removes selfish feelings and action; it creates accountability and installs responsibility. Motivation and dedication come from within your heart and soul, work becomes easier, and the challenges become less daunting.

Your values are your foundation, your passion is what excites, inspires and motivates you, and your purpose is the reason you do what you do, and feel the way you feel. Your why is a combination of all three of these elements. Your Why is your personal mission statement, it is the reason you are willing to run, crawl, sweat, sacrifice, bleed, hurt and continue no matter what. The stronger the why, the better the results. Knowing your why is the single most important influence in achieving your commitments; without it you are just running in circles, and chasing someones elses dreams.

Hint: Serve a higher purpose than yourself. "Whoever renders service to many puts himself in line for greatness—great wealth, great return, great satisfaction, great reputation, and great joy." - Jim Rohn

Serving a higher purpose takes faith, effort and selflessness. It is hard to be upset or feel sorry for yourself when you are serving others.

Colossians 3:22: "Dedicate everything you do to a higher purpose. Everything you do is in glory to God." (Even if it is sweeping the streets.)

- *Activity 9:* Commitment Cards: Now that you have defined your W's, you have the beginning of your commitment card(s). You will eventually have a card for each commitment but for now, pick one of your wants, and write it in the center of a commitment card *(you can use a 3x5 or a 5x7 card).*
- *Step 2: Write down the answer to the following statement (on the top right of the card): Achieving this commitment is important to me because...*
- *Step 3: Write down the answer to the following statement (on the bottom of the back of the card): I am grateful that I have (write down your commitment as if you have achieved it) because it allows me to...*
- *<u>Team:</u> Create team commitment cards. Involve your team members, the more participation, the more invested your team is to each commitment the higher the possibility of success.*
- ***Keep this card close; we will be using them throughout the rest of the book*

WIN:

The WILL to win is one of the most overlooked and undervalued factors in determining success. There is wanting to win, and there is a relentless will to win. They are not the same. <u>Your personal WHY is your will to win</u>. The relentless power of your why is the single most important factor in achieving success. There are times when everything goes to shit—plans, weather, relationships, injuries, etc. Shit happens; but your ability, power and determined will to win is what will get you through it. The most successful people are not the most talented, they are not the most gifted or blessed, they are the most persistent, dedicated and relentless.

REMEMBER YOUR W's.

"Remember who you are, what you are, and who you represent."
- David Rocastle

This is one of my favorite quotes regarding your W's. There is a popular acronym in the sports world: R.W.Y.P.F. (remember who you play for). The team, the community, the school, your family, and yourself are all reason you play, and they are all play an important role in your dedication, actions, mindset, effort and results. The W's take this acronym to another level. R.W.Y.A. (Remember Who, What, Where, When, and Why You Are.) You deserve it, you control it, you can accomplish it; remember, it is up to YOU!

"Character isn't something you were born with and can't change, like your fingerprints. It's something you weren't born with and must take responsibility for forming." - Jim Rohn[1]

Your W's are your fundamentals. Your fundamentals can be improved, expanded, grown and even changed. When you are ready to take control, to be accountable, and to ultimately be a winner, start with your fundamentals, start with your W's. When you struggle, when you feel pressure, anxiety, hopeless or want to quit. Go back to your fundamentals, simplify, focus and recommit. Your W's, those fundamental beliefs, reasons, commitments and ethics will get you through it.

The fundamentals are the first things you are taught when you are learning a new sport or activity. They are the basics that allow you to participate in the event, understand the rules and start to improve. The better you become at those skills the better you are able to perform. Think of a bull rider in a rodeo—he spends countless hours and eventually years learning to hang on and ride that animal. There are basic fundamentals that will help him stay on that bull. Grip, position and posture, balance and core control, timing and movement, free arm and spurring, mental preparation, and dismount technique, just to name a few. If you or I jump on a bull today without any of those fundamentals, how do you think that will go? If an experienced bull rider allows those same basic fundamental skills to faulter or get sloppy, how do you

---

1. *https://www.azquotes.com/author/12558-Jim_Rohn*

think will end up? All these basic skills need to work together to even have a chance to stay on that bull for 8 seconds.

Defining your W's, gives you everything you need to win; you know your desires, your purpose, your fundamental beliefs and the character traits you value the most, you have established a timeline and you know where you started, where you are going, and how far along the journey you are. The only thing left to do is for YOU to get to work. The next chapter is dedicated to that exact thing—we focus on you! You are your biggest strength or your biggest weakness.

Chapter 3: I (You)

The I = I (YOU)

The I is exactly that—it means you! Your beliefs, your thoughts, your actions, your commitments, and your motivations. I am in control of, I am accountable to, I am responsible for, etc. There are so many factors in your life that you cannot control. When you focus on these things you are literally focusing on failure, you are giving yourself permission to stumble, make excuses, and quit. You are allowing yourself to accept an excuse (not my fault, that's out of my control), to accept and settle for less.

Everything is about you! You hear something, read something, or see something and decide that it doesn't apply to you, coach isn't talking about you, that isn't what you do, etc. The truth is that you play an active role in absolutely everything that happens to, through and because of you! When you realize and accept that no matter the situation, outcome or result you had a hand in it. You can execute change and improve. Lose a game on a "bad" call? What plays before that could have been made that would have made that call a non-factor in the game, or prevented that situation from ever arising in the first place? Did you do everything possible to be your best every day in practice, in school, at home, mentally, physically, and emotionally? I can go on and on, but the fact is this: You create and control your reality! Focus on the things you CAN control, Control your Controllables!

THE CONTROLLABLES

"Ability is what you're capable of doing. Motivation determines what you do. Attitude determines how well you do it." - Lou Holtz

Confidence is key to success, it is a vital component in the ability to overcome and persevere through challenges on your way to fulfilling your commitments. Confidence is the feeling of being in control, Pressure is the fear of losing control, and Failure is the feeling of not having control. (You can add depression, low confidence, anxiety, stress, etc. to the list of feelings or fears about not having control. They are all byproducts of us feeling like we are either in control of our lives, our actions, our bodies, and untimely our results, or not.)

Control what you can control, let the rest go. (You can't do anything about it, anyway.) Sports, with its dynamic and unpredictable nature, often mirrors the challenges of life. Athletes face numerous variables, both internal and external, that can impact their performance. In the arena of sports and life, the mastery of controlling what can be controlled is a game-changer. By focusing on aspects within your influence and control, you set yourself on a path to success, no matter the challenges that may arise. In the pursuit of excellence, the art of controlling what can be controlled becomes a crucial aspect of success.

Understanding what is within your control is crucial for maintaining mental and emotional well-being, especially in the face of challenges or uncertainties. While we cannot control everything that happens in our lives, we do have agency over how we react, respond and feel. Controllables are not about talent, they are about preparation, effort, dedication, relentless pursuit, work ethic, and sacrifice. When you are willing to pay that price, you will W.I.N.

The old man and his horse (a Taoist Chinese parable)

Long ago, there was a widowed Chinese farmer. The farmer and his only son labored through the cold winds of winter and scorching rays of summer with their last remaining horse. One day, the son didn't lock the gate of the stable properly, and the horse bolted away.

When neighbors learned what happened, they came to the farmer and said, "What a sadness this is! Without your horse, you'll be unable to maintain the farm. What a failure that your son did not lock the gate properly! This is a great tragedy!"

The farmer replied, "Maybe yes, maybe no."

The next day, the missing horse returned to the farmer's stable, bringing along with it six wild horses. The farmer's son locked the gate of the stable firmly behind all seven horses.

When neighbors learned what happened, they came to the farmer and said, "What happiness this brings! With seven horses, you'll be able to maintain the farm with three of them and sell the rest for huge profits. What a blessing!"

The farmer replied, "Maybe yes, maybe no."

The next day the farmer's son was breaking in one of the wild horses. The son got thrown from the horse, fell hard on rocks, and broke his leg.

When neighbors learned what happened, they came to the farmer and said, "What a great sadness this is! Now, you'll be unable to count on your son's help. What a failure to break in the horse properly! What a tragedy!"

The farmer replied, "Maybe yes, maybe no."

The next day, a general from the Imperial Chinese Army arrived to conscript all the young men of the village into the army. Their assignment was to fight on the front lines of a battle against a terrifying enemy of overwhelming force. The farmer's son, because of his broken leg, was not taken.

When neighbors learned what happened, they came to the farmer and said, "What a great joy! Your son avoided facing certain death on the front lines of the battle. What a blessing!"

The farmer replied, "Maybe yes, maybe no."

We have no way of knowing if an apparent challenge, trial, or hardship is a blessing in our lives until we go through it. The old famer couldn't change the situation or control the outcome, he could only control his attitude moving forward. Don't focus on the things you can't control, stop worrying, and trying to understand things you will never understand, focus on the potential learning, growth, or unforeseen blessings of a challenge and keep moving forward in control of you.

Below is a small list of a few of the most common controllables. You will have others that you add to your personal list, and you will come across some that you feel like you may not have complete control over; this allows you to identify areas to focus on and improve. It also identifies potential areas of pressure and stress that you may not have been able to pinpoint where it was coming from.

Attitude: *"Even though we can't always choose our circumstances, we can always choose our attitude in the circumstances." – Tony Dungy*

Everything starts and ends with attitude and if you get it right, all else will fall in line with it. You can control your attitude in all places and at all times. You can choose to have a positive attitude in the face of adversity or during a task that you don't really want to be doing but is necessary. To keep a positive attitude, find a benefit in everything you do. Identify how every task, no matter how small, contributes to you accomplishing your commitments.

Intentional: *"I fear not the man who has practiced 10,000 kicks once, but I fear the man who has practiced one kick 10,000 times." - Bruce Lee*

Set out with intention and be intentional in all you do; if you are going to take the time to do something, make it worth it. When you are intentional in your commitments, energy, and actions, everything you do moves you a step closer to achieving your commitments. Activities done with the right intention develop and form habits that carry over into every aspect of your life and success. How you do anything is how you do everything!

Effort: *"There's only one way to succeed in anything, and that is to give everything." -Bill Parcells*

Effort is more powerful than talent. Effort doesn't quit, it is relentless in its pursuit of the commitment. Talent is like a fire, it is powerful, but if you don't feed it, it will die. Effort is like water; it might take time, but eventually it will cut through stone. The Grand Canyon has been carved over millions of years as the Colorado River cuts down through the plateau with consistent, relentless effort. How hard you work is up to you and no one else. PERIOD!

Preparation: *"Pressure is something you feel when you don't know what the hell you're doing." - Peyton Manning*

Meticulous preparation is within your control. Preparation equips you to face the challenges of competition, and life. Preparation is the basis of confidence, and confidence overcomes pressure and fear.

Motivation: *"To succeed...You need to find something to hold on to, something to motivate you, something to inspire you." - Tony Dorsett*

A key component of success is your ability to control your motivation. Motivation can be found in anything and everything around you—in commercials, on social media, in school, books, at work or at home, in nature or in the most seemingly insignificant of tasks and activities. Being and doing your best in all that you do is strictly speaking motivation enough for anything you do.

<u>Physical Health:</u> *"If you don't do what's best for your body, you're the one who comes up on the short end." – Julius Erving*

Your ability to perform is directly impacted by your food and hydration choices as well as the amount of rest and sleep you get. Fueling your body with the right nutrients and rest contribute to physical, mental, and emotional well-being. Weight training, stretching, and cardio are just as important as skill development to your success.

<u>Adaptability:</u> *"The only true limitation is the one you set for yourself." - Usain Bolt*

You cannot control external factors; however, you can control how you respond to those factors (e.g., weather, officiating, injuries, other's opinions of us, etc.). Adaptability to adjust to unexpected challenges is a skill that distinguishes the elite and the ultra- successful.

<u>Teamwork</u>: *"Teamwork is so important that it is virtually impossible for you to reach the heights of your capabilities or make the money that you want without becoming very good at it." — Brian Tracy*

No one accomplishes anything alone. It takes a team to accomplish greatness. You might be the only one on the mat for the match, but you had a team with you training, you had coaches pushing and teaching you, you have people that support and believe in you. We are all part of a team. You have control over our contributions to the team dynamics. Communication, collaboration, and a positive attitude are all aspects within your control and influence.

<u>Dedication:</u> *"We all have dreams. But in order to make dreams come into reality, it takes an awful lot of determination, dedication, self-discipline, and effort." -* ***Jesse Owens***

Dedication is motivation on steroids. It is the internal drive that prompts you to act. It is the quality of being committed and devoted to a task, purpose, or goal with unwavering determination and effort. Dedication is characterized by a willingness to put in the necessary time and energy, even in the face of obstacles or challenges, to achieve a desired outcome. It reflects a deep passion and a sense of responsibility towards fulfilling one's commitments and aspirations. It requires a strong sense of loyalty and persistence, accompanied by hard work, discipline, and sacrifice. It plays a crucial role in influencing behavior, enhancing performance, and achieving success.

<u>Discipline:</u> *"If you have discipline, you can do anything". -Bill Parcells*

Failure is only achieved when you quit. Discipline is the ability to carry out a decision after the emotion of making the decision has passed. It is easy to have a moment of motivation or inspiration to accomplish something great; it is much harder to see it through the tough times, the challenges and the trials. If you have the discipline to never quit, to do whatever it takes to be successful...you will be.

<u>Communication:</u> *"If you just communicate, you can get by. But if you communicate skillfully, you can work miracles." – Jim Rohn*

Positive, assertive, and clear communication is vital for success. Clear communication begins with the way we talk to and about ourselves. Positive self-talk is a powerful tool in achieving success. *I can, I will, and I am* are empowering words that need to be in your daily communication with yourself and with others.

<u>Body Language</u>: *"What you do speaks so loud that I cannot hear what you say." –Ralph Waldo Emerson*

One of the most visible and easiest things you have control over. Confident body language sends a clear and powerful message to your teammates, your coaches, your opponents, and yourself. You are in control!

<u>Emotions:</u> *"Emotion can be the enemy, if you give into your emotion, you lose yourself. You must be at one with your emotions, because the body always follows the mind."–Bruce Lee*

Controlling your emotions is the epitome of self-control. Emotional responses and reactions are directly related to your feelings and understanding of control in the moment.

Those who manage stress, anxiety, and frustration effectively are better positioned to make sound decisions during competition and high stress situations. Emotional regulation is the key contributor to mental resilience a positive mindset, and success.

<u>Commitment:</u> *"There's a difference between interest and commitment. When you're interested in doing something, you do it only when it's convenient. When*

you're committed to something, you accept no excuses – only results." – Ken Blanchard

Commitment is constant thought, loyalty, dedication and an unrelenting pursuit of a result, promise or passion.

<u>Focus:</u> " *"The successful warrior is the average man, with laser-like focus." -Bruce Lee*

Concentrating on your commitments, your goals and your "why's" will eventually filter out irrelevant distractions and amplify what aligns with your current commitments. By focusing on your commitments, you are training your mind to remove all distractions and influences that are contrary to achieving that outcome.

<u>Mindset:</u> *"The people who are crazy enough to think they can change the world are the ones who do." -Steve Jobs*

Mindset is a powerful determinant of success. Maintaining a positive and focused mindset, regardless of external circumstances, and influences is key. Having a belief in your abilities and focusing on the present moment, you are setting the stage for success. Develop a mindset of everything you do, can and will benefit you and move you closer to achieving success and accomplishing your commitments. A determined, positive mindset = success.

<u>Coachability:</u> *"My best skill was that I was coachable. I was a sponge and aggressive to learn." - Michael Jordan*

Your ability to receive, accept, and apply the coaching, advice, and council you receive. Being coachable starts and ends with accountability and responsibility. You can always learn; you can always improve.

<u>Ego/Pride:</u> *"You are never really playing an opponent. You are playing yourself, your own highest standards, and when you reach your limits, that is real joy." - Arthur Ashe*

Your ego/pride has profound impact on your perceptions, distorting your reality and influencing how you interpret events, interactions, and feedback. When ego and pride are dominant, individuals perceive themselves as infallible, invulnerable, or superior to others, leading to a sense of entitlement and a reluctance to acknowledge weaknesses. Keep your ego in check, focusing on improving yourself daily, rather than being superior to others.

<u>Breathing:</u> *"Your breath holds the key to unlocking your physical and mental potential." -Patrick McKeown (The Oxygen Advantage)*

Controlled, focused and purposeful breathing offers numerous benefits for physical, mental, and emotional well-being. Physically, it improves oxygenation, lung function, heart health, and pain management. Mentally, it reduces stress, enhances focus, and improves sleep quality. Emotionally, it helps manage anxiety, regulate mood, and increase emotional resilience. Overall, controlled breathing strengthens the mind-body connection, boosts immunity, and enhances athletic and mental performance.

<u>Gratitude:</u> *"He is a wise man who does not grieve for the things which he has not but rejoices for those which he has." – Epictetus*

It is very easy to get caught up in the negatives of life—the things you don't have, the things that didn't go how you wanted them to, the advantages others have, even the weather, etc. This practice will affect absolutely everything you do if you allow it into your life. You are blessed, you are gifted, you are loved the more you focus on the positive the more positive will be in your life. Start with daily focus and acknowledgment of the good things in your life. Begin everyday with 3 things you are grateful for in your life—family, job, hobbies, success, love, experience, trials, lessons, weather, home, animals, etc. The list is HUGE. End every day with a list of 3 things you were grateful for that day! Gratitude directly effects attitude! If you want to install a positive attitude it starts with gratitude.

<u>YOU:</u> *"You can't always control circumstances. However, you can always control your attitude, approach, and response. Your options are to complain or to look ahead and figure out how to make the situation better." - Tony Dungy*

You are your greatest controllable. You can be better today than you were yesterday, and better the day after that etc. External circumstances and challenges can feel overwhelming, but the one constant is your ability to control your actions, mindset, and effort. Your dedication to preparation, your commitments, character, and the honesty with which you evaluate your progress is entirely within your power. By taking ownership of your choices and responses to setbacks, you position yourself to overcome and succeed. Embracing this truth empowers you to consistently push your boundaries, adapt to new challenges, and strive toward your highest potential. Ultimately, the most significant influence on your outcomes isn't luck, talent, or the actions of others, it's your commitment to always doing, giving and being your best.

Controllables are not God-given talents that you are born with, they are skills and attributes that can be developed, improved, and mastered. Controlling your Controllables is a key element to success. There are hundreds of controllables in your life and in every situation. I have only listed a few of the more general and broader controllable factors in your life. Learn to identify those elements in times of challenges, pressure and anxiety that you have control over, and you will overcome those negative feelings, thoughts and anxiety and triumph to win. The Serenity Prayer says it best, "God grant me the serenity to accept the things I cannot change, the courage to change the things, I can, and the wisdom to know the difference."

Activity 10:

- *Part I: Review activity 7 and write down your 10-15 controllables for each of your commitments. There will be some factors that you will always have control of and in some cases; there will be different things that you can control based on your position, title, responsibilities, etc. It is important to identify your controllables for each commitment.*

- *Part II: Pick the 5 most important controllables for achieving this commitment and write them on your commitment card (on the top left of the front of the card).*

- *Part II: Gratitude statements. List 5 things you are grateful for in relation to your commitment and write them on your commitment card (front, bottom left of the card).*

- *<u>Team:</u> Complete each part of this activity as a team. Individuals will have their own lists and statements as well, but it is important to have team controllables and gratitude statements. These lists are a great tool when concerns or complaints like playing time, attendance, effort, are brought up during the season.*

MAKE IT HAPPEN, OR LET IT HAPPEN, ITS YOUR CHOICE.

"Some people want it to happen, some wish it would happen, and others make it happen."- Michael Jordan

There are only 2 options in life: you can either make it happen or you can let it happen. Identifying your controllables gives you the power to make it happen. Excuses are born from lack of control or the lack of feeling in control. It happens to you; you don't have the power to stop it from happening or it is someone or something else's fault is the victim mentality. That attitude and perception is a commitment killer and success suicide. You have the power to make anything happen, the question is never if you have the control to make it happen the question is always this: Are you willing to make it happen?

The Pack Mentality or peer pressure is a very real and powerful force in your life. The desire to be liked, respected and appreciated is one of the most influential forces in your life, many times without consciously realizing it, you settle for less just to stay with the pack. If you get out in front there is always a target on your back, if you get to far behind, you are left. Your comfort zone is right in the middle of the pack. You don't have to make tough choices; you follow the pack. You don't have to be alone; you follow the pack. You don't have to be in control; you follow the pack. Success is not earned or attained from the middle of the pack; you must be willing to lead, and to venture off on your own and risk the pack leaving you if you want to W.I.N.

The truth is that you are rarely out of control, you are in fact not willing to take control. Control comes with responsibility, accountability, and dependability. Those three abilities are powerful, but they are also the things that keeps most people from making it happen. It is easier to blame others, and to settle for 2nd, 3rd or 35th then to try and fail. Be responsible for your thoughts, be accountable for your actions and be dependable with your effort and you will have control of your success.

META-COMMUNICATION

"Effective communication is 20% what you know and 80% how you feel about what you know." –Jim Rohn

How you talk to yourself is a life-or-death situation for your goals, aspirations, and commitments. It directly impacts your success or failure. Positive self-talk is a key contributor to confidence, resilience, and success. Learning to incorporate and effectively use self-talk practices in your life will reap great rewards but there is another level beyond self-talk. I call it Meta-Com or meta-communication.

Meta-COM involves self-communication on four distinct levels: verbal, non-verbal physical, non-verbal mental, and emotional. Each level represents a different way in which we interact with and understand ourselves.

1. Verbal: This involves the internal dialogue that takes place in your mind, often referred to as self-talk. It includes the words, phrases, and affirmations you consciously or unconsciously say to yourself. Verbal self-communication can be positive or negative, and it plays a significant role in shaping your self-perception and behavior. It's the most direct way to communicate with yourself, often reflecting your beliefs, thoughts, and attitudes.

2. Non-Verbal Physical: Non-verbal physical self-communication encompasses the ways in which your body language, posture, facial expressions, and other physical gestures communicate messages to yourself and others. This level involves how your physical state reflects and influences your internal state. For instance, standing tall with your shoulders back can reinforce a sense of confidence, while slouching might convey (and perpetuate) feelings of insecurity. This form of communication is subtle but powerful, often operating on a subconscious level and influencing your emotions and mental state as well as those around you.

3. Non-Verbal Mental: Non-verbal mental self-communication involves the imagery, visualizations, and unspoken thoughts that occur in your mind. It includes the mental pictures you create, the scenarios you imagine, and the abstract concepts or ideas you contemplate. This level of communication is more abstract and symbolic, allowing you to process complex emotions, plan, and problem-solve without relying on words. For example, visualizing yourself successfully completing a task can boost motivation and reduce anxiety.

4. Emotional: Emotional self-communication refers to the way you interpret and understand your own emotions. It involves recognizing, labeling, and processing feelings, as well as how you respond to these emotions internally. This level of communication helps you to connect with your emotional state, making it possible to regulate your feelings and respond to them in a healthy way. For instance, acknowledging feelings of frustration and understanding their source allows you to manage them constructively. Emotional self-communication is key to emotional intelligence and plays a crucial role in overall well-being.

Together, these four levels of self-communication create a dynamic and holistic process that forms the foundation of the Meta-Com. By becoming aware of and actively engaging with each level, you can cultivate a deeper understanding of yourself, leading to greater self-awareness, self-control, personal growth, and success.

Neuro-Linguistic Programming (NLP) is a method that helps you naturally reprogram your mind by recognizing how the words you speak, think, and hear (meta-communication) profoundly influences your mindset, motivation, and performance. Defining your W's established the foundation for your NLP focus. Your list is written in direct, defined and positive language. Those words and phrases are in fact able to change the way your brain "thinks" about yourself. By using powerful, intentional and clear language you are programming your brain to focus on the positive talents, commitments, skills and dedication you have! The elite athletes and ultra successful have mastered the principles and practices of Meta-Com and use it daily, in fact, they use it multiple times a day.

Activity 11:

- *1: Stand in front of the mirror and look at yourself, look at your face, your eyes, your smile. Speak out loud the first 3 thoughts you have.*
- *Write them Down.*
- *2: Look at your body, and your clothes, your posture.*
- *Speak out loud the first 3 thoughts you have.*
- *Write them Down.*

- *Review your comments. Were they positive, motivational, confident, and forward focused or were they negative, mean or even hurtful? Were your eyes alive with excitement or are they dull? Were you smiling? How about your posture? Shoulders back? Head up? Were you dressed for success? How you think, feel, act, and talk to and about yourself is a powerful push in a direction, which way are you pushing yourself?*

- **If you had negative thought and comments, rewrite them into positive, inspiring, motivation comments. Wash your face, comb your hair, brush your teeth, put on clothes appropriate for your activities today.*

- *Now repeat steps one and 2 but use the new comments. Do this over and over until you can see your physical appearance improve, your posture will improve, your eyes will light up, and you will smile at the possibilities of who you are, where your headed and what you will accomplish.*

- ***If you had positive thoughts and comments for yourself, Great Job. Now go out and get to work!*

<u>Team:</u> Review your team posture and culture. When you and your team members talk about the program, the team, the individual members, etc., what is the overall feeling? What is the outlook for the upcoming season? Are you working to change a negative culture, improve a current culture, or maintain a winning culture? Do your team members feel like they are a part of the team or a spectator looking in? Do you have good team chemistry? Has your team bought into your direction, culture, and commitments? Create lists, discuss the negative or challenging comments, and as a team, identify and commit to making changes and how you will implement those changes.

I AM

The most powerful word in the world is "I". I am, I will, I can, I do, I believe. Those are all powerful, accountable, responsible, and empowering statements. Your language has the power to shape your reality. The words you choose to describe yourself and your experiences will either limit you or set you free. I AM statements increase confidence. When you repeatedly declare statements such as "I am capable," "I am deserving," or "I am worthy," you strengthen your self-perception and cultivate a deep sense of self-worth. By reinforcing positive beliefs, you become more resilient in the face of challenges and more open to seizing opportunities. I AM statements are not merely empty words. When combined with intention and emotion, they become powerful tools for manifestation, and remind you of your aspirations, helping you stay focused and motivated. Being your I AM statement will lead you to accomplish your commitments. They are direct reflections of each other. Your I AM statement is the realization of your commitment in the present tense.

Creating an I Am statement does you no good if you don't put it to regular use. Implementing your I AM statements into your daily routine is crucial to its success. It is important for you to hear yourself say these statements out loud, so repeat them at least five times per day. In moments of challenges, self-doubt, trial and struggle, repeating your I AM statements provide clarity of your commitments and reaffirm your self-worth and abilities. *Hint: The effectiveness of affirmations lies in their authenticity and consistency. When you choose the affirmations that resonate with you personally and repeat them multiple times a day with genuine belief and energy, they will profoundly impact your self-perception and your results.*

Activity 12: I AM / AFFIRMATION STATEMENT

Review activity 11. Those are examples of positive affirmation statements; however, the most effective statements don't come from rewriting negative thoughts or comments but from creating a statement of purpose with powerful calls to action and commitments to yourself, family, team, and purpose.

1. Start with the End in Mind: Think about the specific area of your life where you want to create change. What goal or personal quality do you want to focus on? (For example, if you want more confidence: "I am confident in every situation.")

2. Use the Present Tense: (Example: Instead of "I want to be healthy," say "I am vibrant, healthy, and full of energy.")

3. Affirmations should always be positive: Focus on what you do want, rather than what you want to avoid. (Example: Instead of saying "I am not stressed," say "I am calm, centered, and in control.")

4. Make It Personal: Tailor your affirmations to reflect your unique desires and goals. The more personal and specific your affirmations, the more powerful they are.

5. Keep It Short and Simple: Your affirmations should be short, simple, and easy to remember.

6. Repeat Your Affirmations multiple times daily, especially in moments of doubt or when you feel the need for a boost. I highly recommend starting everyday with your affirmation statements.

Hint: Review your "WHO" and write down the top traits you want to have, create and be. Write 3-5 simple statements that begin with "I am" and complete the statements. Keep these statements as short and memorable as possible. Affirmation statements are a transformative process. By aligning your thoughts and words with the person you want to become, and the goals you want to achieve, you empower yourself to take the necessary steps toward accomplishing those commitments; Remember, change doesn't happen overnight, but with persistence, positive beliefs will take root and flourish.

**Creating and utilizing affirmation statements with your family, your team, and your peers has the same effect but also unites you together in a common purpose and commitment. Affirmation statements are often used privately and individually but the power of positive affirmation multiplies as you include, adopt, and enroll additional supporters.*

Team: As a team, follow the steps above and create a team Affirmation Statement, WE ARE....

Chapter 4: N = Non-Negotiables

The N is for Non-negotiables.

In an interview with Jay Shetty, Kobe Bryant was asked how he keeps up with his insane training schedule, starting as early as 4:00 a.m. and consisting of 4-6 sessions of 2-4 hours per session, 6 days a week. His response is one of the greatest examples of non- negotiables I have come across. *I'm not negotiating with myself...I signed that contract with myself. I'm doing it."*

Kobe goes on to explain his reasoning behind the brutal training schedule. *"If you want to be a great player, if you play every single day 2, 3 hours, every single day, over the course of a year, how much better are you getting? Most kids will play maybe an hour and a half two days a week. Do the math on that. That's not gonna get it done. Not gonna get it done."*

Once you have set your commitment(s) and you have established you are accountable and in control, it's time to get to work. That is the non-negotiables. The work, the sacrifice, and effort. The strength of your non-negotiables will determine the strength of your ability to follow through with your commitment(s) and the level of success you will achieve.

Non-negotiables:

"There is never a right time to do the wrong thing and there is never a wrong time to do the right thing" -Lou Holtz

Your non-negotiables are the things that are important to you, the things you expect from yourself, and the things you are not willing to compromise on. These are the things that no matter the circumstance or situation you will do, no matter what, you WILL stay true to these things. (Examples are no drugs or alcohol, make 100 free throws in a row daily. Practice, training, rest, grades, and studies are all positive non-negotiables.) Keep your non-negotiables positive (<u>do</u> rather, that <u>not do</u>), removing negative talk, thoughts, and actions is a major contributor to your success. The words we think and speak have a direct influence on your thoughts, motivations, emotions, action, and success. Focus on the positive. Think, feel, act, and speak positive and you will be positive.

You are making a contract with yourself. We, as humans, are, by nature, selfish and lazy; even the way our brain works is lazy. Our brain looks to automate tasks to reduce the amount of energy and time expended on any task. We call these habits. Once we have learned a task and completed it several times, our brain begins to create a repetitive process or habit to make this task simple and reduce the energy spent on each task of our day. Creating a list of non-negotiables establishes a baseline "habitual belief or response." If you have already decided the answer to a question, reaction to a situation, or response to stimuli, then your brain will, in turn, create a habit associated with that preprogramed response. Your non-negotiables are based on your W's. Thoughts = Actions = Habits = Character.

Commitment and effort are physical, mental, and emotional. Are you giving your best effort physically, emotionally, mentally and spiritually? Do not negotiate with yourself. Set your non-negotiables and do not waiver from them for anything or anyone that is less important than your commitments or out of alignment with your W's.

- I will always:
- Be on time
- Give my best effort

- Respect others (not belittle, make fun or speak ill about another person)
- Be willing to learn
- Be honest (no cheating, stealing, lying)
- Eat healthy
- Train 6 days a week
- Daily prayer
- Keep my body clean (no alcohol, drugs, smoking or vaping)
- Keep my mind clear (no pornography, hateful music, etc.)
- Read daily to train my mind

These are just a few examples of non-negotiables and how to state them in a positive manner. Make your own list, post it where you will read it and say it daily. Do NOT negotiate with yourself. Once you have made a commitment, it is law. Allowing yourself even the slightest margin for negotiation, the tiniest sliver of doubt, laziness, and minimalized effort will fester until it infects your entire commitment with negative thoughts, actions, half-ass effort or questionable mindset and attitude. <u>Your commitments are non-negotiable</u>.

Activity 13: I WILL

Step 1: Review activity 10 and below your list of controllables for each commitment. Write the words "I WILL."

Step 2: List 5-10 of your non-negotiables that apply to each commitment. (Example: I WILL: Do my best, be on time, be honest, drink 60oz of water per day, etc.). Remember to keep them positive for example: I will be on time, rather than I will not be late. Always focus on positive goals, positive thoughts, actions, emotions and speech.)

Step 3: Choose the top 5 non-negotiables and write them on the bottom right of your commitment cards with the title: "I WILL."

<u>*Team:*</u> *As a team follow the steps above and fill in the top 5 non-negotiables for your team.*

WHAT LEVEL ARE YOU?

"I'm a big believer in the idea that you don't rise to the occasion, you sink to the level of your training." - MIKE TOMLIN.

There are multiple levels to everything you do. If you are in situation that you are excited about, you are motivated to win, you will give a higher effort in that moment then when you are asked to do a chore or task you don't like or appreciate. Practice is like this for most people, practice isn't a game, so it doesn't matter as much, or you will pick it up when it matters (in the game). How you do anything is how you do everything! Can you give more effort at a particular time than another? Yes, however if you haven't invested your best effort leading up to that moment you have put a cap on the level that your momentary effort can reach. If you are lazy with your schoolwork, job, or chores; you will be lazy with your training! If you are lazy with your training; you are lazy for your performance. Think of your daily activities on a scale of 1-10. This is anything and everything you do on any given day: make your bed, go to school or work, do chores, run errands, interact with your friends and family, hobbies, training, education, practice, anything and everything. All these tasks are scored 1-10 (10 being your best). If you constantly perform those sometime mundane tasks at a level 6. Your body is trained and prepared for a level 6 effort and a level 6 result. You limit your ability to perform at a higher level if you never practice or train at that higher level. Everything you do and how you do it matters.

Motivation vs. Dedication:

The biggest difference between motivation and dedication is ACTION. Motivation is the initiative to start a task; it is a momentary dopamine spike or energy and excitement, it is being led, pushed or pulled by outside stimuli. Dedication goes beyond a mere desire. It is your commitment to following through with behaviors and actions that will lead to the accomplishment of that commitment (goal). In other words, motivation does not require action because it is purely an inner desire. Dedication, on the other hand, is both internal and and hard work. Dedication is relentless, it doesn't stop; fear, rain, snow, heat, ridicule, challenges and setbacks are just speed bumps to the dedicated.

There are two primary motivational forces: love and fear. They both play pivotal roles in shaping our decisions, behaviors, and ultimately, the results we achieve. How we choose to interpret, react, and use those forces shapes our character.

Love-based motivation involves pursuing commitments driven by passion, purpose, and a genuine desire for growth, contribution, and service to others. Love-based motivations cultivate deeper connections, purpose-driven actions, and sustainable growth, enhancing overall well-being and fostering positive relationships with yourself and others. When you are motivated by love, you become dedicated to the activity, it becomes part of your purpose. Love based motivation is dedication.

Fear-based motivation, stems from the desire to avoid negative outcomes, consequences, or threats, often driven by anxiety, insecurity, or external pressures. Relying solely on fear leads to stress, burnout, and a lack of fulfillment and commitment in the long run.

Both love and fear drive human behavior; the most fulfilling and sustainable motivation stems from a place of love, passion, and purpose (dedication). Through dedication, embracing the power of love, and following your purpose, you will unleash your full potential and the full potential of others. Understanding your purpose and your motivation (dedication) to your purpose is the secret to continued relentless effort in the face of challenges. When you are dedicated, you cannot and will not fail.

Expectation vs. Commitment:

Expectations are not reality; they are not even goals. They are dreams, they are unrealized potential. Expectation is a thought, a desire, a belief, or a hope. Expectation is the opposite of commitment. Commitment requires effort, loyalty, dedication and work. We all have expectations for performance and results in the activities and tasks we undertake. We have expectations of what we hope, wish, or think will happen, but the reality is expectations are not reality or success. If you want to WIN, you must be committed.

Do your expectations match your commitment? Your performance is direct reflection of your commitment.

A close friend's son was a freshman in high school and was a very good wrestler. He had a goal of winning a state championship his freshman year and a higher goal to be a 4-time state wrestling champion. During the state tournament he lost a very close and tough match to a superior opponent. He wrestled tough, he gave his best effort at that time in that match, but he ultimately lost that match. His goal of winning a state championship and being a 4-time state champion were both gone. He was obviously upset, and tears flowed. His coach said to him, "You are not good enough to cry!" Talk about tough love. There are only 2 choices in that moment. The first option is to be offended, be upset, and mad. The second option is to listen to your coach, self-scout, and ask yourself if you had done everything you could have. In reality, the wrestler realized that while he did give his best effort in the match, he had not given his best effort during the time leading up to that match. He didn't make it to the gym for all the offseason training and workouts, he missed a few of the early morning practices, he skipped through the mental training and journaling, and he didn't go 100% in every practice. That season he settled for good rather than do what it took to be great.

That day, his goals became commitments, and he went on to win three straight state championships as an individual and as a team. He became a team captain, and that commitment and effort carried over into his leadership and example in his other sports, schooling, and activities. His coach wasn't referring to his actual skill level when he said you're not good enough to cry, he was referring to his commitment, his effort during the entire year, not just in that moment. Are you committed? Are you good enough to cry? Does your expectation match your commitment? Everyone wants to win, everyone practices, and some do extra, but it's the elite, the very few that are truly committed.

Desperation vs. Determination:

Desperation is fear, anxiety, and a lack of options, resulting in erratic actions, impulsive decisions, and a focus on short-term solutions. It is marked by a sense of helplessness and losing control, often leading to mistakes and negative outcomes. When you are desperate for something, you are at its mercy, it is in control of your thoughts, decisions and actions. Desperation destroys purpose. Determination is strength, resolve, and dedication, leading to consistent effort, strategic planning, and long-term success. Determination sees a wall and climbs over; Determination knows that impossible is actually saying I-M-Possible. Determination doesn't make excuses it doesn't waver, and it never quits. Don't be so desperate for anything that you will trade everything.

Cost vs. Value:

In your relentless pursuit of your commitments and goals, you will often find yourselves grappling with the balance between cost and value. If you could experience the feeling, the joy, the sense of accomplishment, the admiration, the surge of energy and the power of living the life you want, of not only achieving but exceeding your goals and commitments, if you could experience that for even one day, you would never stop until you reached that feeling again. There is a cost to everything in life, to be great at something you must pay a price, there is a required imbalance of time, effort, dedication, focus, money, etc. Ask yourself, are you willing to pay the price or is the cost too high? Do you set goals and commitments based on the value or based on the cost? Value has no concern for the cost. If it is valuable to you, you will pay it, if the cost is too great, you won't. When you are consumed only with the cost, you will settle for less. You eat chicken instead of steak, you get water instead of wine. Know your value, know the value of your destination, and do not settle for less because of cost. Be willing to pay the price to achieve the value that you deserve.

Hunger vs. Appetite:

Hunger is a need; it is your body responding to the requirement for nutrients to survive. Appetite is a desire; it is a want. Are you hungry to accomplish your commitments or are they more of an appetite in your life? When you are hungry and starving, you will do anything for food. You will choose food over any other want in that moment. The same level of hunger (need) is required if you want to accomplish your commitments. Ask yourself, am I hungry for this (insert desire, want or commitment)? If you are hungry and stay hungry even when you get a little taste of your commitment, then I am excited to see your success, because you will WIN.

A young man asked Socrates to show him the path to wisdom, and Socrates instructed him to meet at the river at dawn. There, Socrates led the man into the water, repeatedly submerging him and asking what he wanted. Initially, the man said he sought wisdom, but as he was held underwater longer, thirty seconds passed, then forty, and the man's face began to turn blue. Socrates lifted the man up and asked, "What do you want?" The man gasped, "Air!" Socrates released the young man and said, "When you want wisdom as much as you have just wanted air, then you will begin to find wisdom." The pursuit of your commitments must be as intense and essential as your need for air.

Momentum vs. Control:

Momentum is fake; it is made up in your mind. You are going to struggle, you are going to have challenges, and you are going to face adversity in your life, in your relationships, your family, your job, and your sport. When these things happen it is not the work of some force that wants you to fail, because you are unworthy of success, happiness, or winning. They are just the steps to learning, growing, and improving. Momentum is you allowing your mind to control your emotions, and actions. You allow yourself to feel like you are losing control, raising your stress level, increasing your respiratory rate, and turning up the pressure valve. Momentum is nothing more than your perception of the situation, change your perception and you will change your attitude and your results.

Setting your commitments, identifying your controllables, and establishing your non-negotiables is literally reprogramming your mindset. Our brains are like massive computers, and sometimes we have so many windows and apps open that we get distracted, and overloaded with information and processes etc. Learning to reset your computer (your mindset). Is vital to your productivity, focus and success. Control is the opposite of momentum. Do not rely on or blame an imaginary outside force to control you. Are you at the mercy of momentum or do you control your perception, attitude, effort and performance?

Truthful vs. Wishful:

"The best are the best because they tell the truth. They tell the truth about who they are, how they prepare, how they work, how they get ready to play, how they push themselves to be the best, the passion that they have to be the best, and they do it all the time." -Nick Saban

A fundamental truth about winning is that it begins with honesty. The best individuals consistently tell the truth about their abilities, preparation, work ethic, and dedication to excellence. They acknowledge both their strengths and weaknesses, understanding that honesty is key to continuous improvement. By telling yourself the truth about who you are and how you operate, you set a clear path for growth and are better positioned to take actionable steps toward your commitments. This level of self-awareness and transparency is what separates the best from the rest.

Honesty in self-scoutingis crucial for success because it helps identify gaps in preparation and effort, allowing for focused improvement. The best individuals constantly push past their comfort zones and hold themselves to high standards, not just occasionally but consistently. This relentless pursuit of excellence, driven by honest self-assessment, fosters accountability, ensures necessary adjustments are made, and ultimately enables them to reach their highest potential. On the other hand, wishful thinking—overestimating capabilities or lying to oneself—can lead to complacency, missed opportunities for growth, and underperformance when it matters most. Embracing truth over wishfulness allows individuals to approach their goals with clarity, commitment, and the willingness to put in the hard work required to succeed.

Being truthful and honest with yourself in self-scouting brings numerous benefits, including enhanced self-awareness, realistic goal setting, increased accountability, and improved resilience. By clearly understanding your strengths and weaknesses, you create a more accurate and actionable plan for growth. This honesty also translates into stronger personal and professional relationships as it builds trust and respect from others. Overall, being truthful with yourself leads to more effective personal development, greater success in achieving your goals, and a stronger sense of confidence in your abilities. Embracing honesty in every aspect of your journey, from preparation to performance, creates a culture of accountability and excellence, paving the way for lasting achievement and fulfillment.

Discipline vs. Regret:

Discipline is a momentary decision for a long-term reward. Regret is the everlasting pain that comes from reflecting on those moments when you chose instant gratification over long term happiness and success. WIN is to exercise discipline and minimize regret in all aspects of your life. Life is a journey a series of choices, each steering you down different paths with varying outcomes. Discipline guides your actions towards long-term goals, while regret often stems from choices made in the moment or lack of action. Discipline is the key to personal growth and success, rooted in consistent, intentional choices that align with your long-term goals. By setting clear commitments and adhering to structured plans, you maintain focus and resilience despite distractions or obstacles. Daily habits like managing time, finances, and self-improvement contribute to steady progress, transforming aspirations into reality by bridging the gap between intention and action. Regret, on the other hand, stems from choices that prioritize short-term satisfaction or neglect long-term goals. While it can teach valuable lessons about aligning with your values, regret can also become a source of stagnation if not addressed constructively. By embracing discipline and making mindful choices, you minimize future regrets and steer your life toward desired outcomes. Learning from past regrets without dwelling on them allows for personal growth and a renewed commitment to long-term success. By prioritizing discipline and making thoughtful choices, you will navigate life's challenges with a greater sense of purpose and satisfaction, ultimately reducing the weight of regret and fostering a more fulfilling journey and outcome.

Discipline and love are deeply intertwined, as both require setting boundaries, providing structure, and guiding you toward your potential. Hard coaching or firm parenting can be seen as acts of love because they are rooted in the desire to foster growth, resilience, and long-term success. By holding athletes (children, teammates, peers, employees, etc.) accountable, pushing them beyond their comfort zones, and maintaining high standards, parents and coaches teach discipline, which ultimately benefits your development. Though it may feel tough in the moment, this discipline fosters independence and emotional growth, teaching you to navigate life with strength and integrity. Hard training and high standards are a form of discipline that shows love by prioritizing your future success over temporary ease. It teaches perseverance, focus, and the importance of effort, ultimately preparing you for greater challenges in life, and for the ultimate commitment of helping you become your best you. Discipline is the ultimate sign of love, it reflects a deep commitment to the well- being and growth of yourself and others. One of the hardest things for a mentor, coach parent and leader to do is discipline the people they love and respect. Everyone wants to be loved, admired and appreciated, rather than being seen as the mean, grumpy bad guy. Loving someone enough to let them hate you while they go through the process of learning, and figuring out that you have their best interest in mind is the ultimate sacrifice of love and respect for others. Be open to hard coaching, be grateful someone cares enough to show you discipline, attention and love.

"I hated every minute of training, but I said, 'Don't quit. Suffer now and live the rest of your life as a champion." – Muhammad Ali

Practice vs. Game:

Everyone wants to play on game day, not everyone wants to practice, and even fewer want to practice hard. How many practices are there per week? Per month, per season, or per year? The answer to these questions might vary a little depending on your sport but the ratio tends to hold true of 4-1. Four practices to every game; that means you have 4 times the number of opportunities to show yourself, your teammates and your coaches that you are game level prepared and ready. Do you take advantage of those opportunities? Do you take on all your tasks, like practice or like a game? Do you prepare for you day like its practice or is it game time? Your level of interest, effort, dedication, preparation and focus is different for practice than a game. If you want to perform at a high level in the game, you must perform at a high level in practice, if you want to perform at a high level in practice make every day gameday!

Accountable vs. Responsible:

A very common response to a mistake, result, or other negative or unanticipated result is "I'M SORRY", or to be a little more with the times "MY Bad". In sports you will often see an athlete tap their chest or point to themselves after a negative play or result to signal my fault, my mistake, my bad and/or I am sorry. These are all common and acceptable responses to a negative outcome. Thy are all examples being accountable.

Accountability is the first step in making significant changes in your results and in your life. However, if you stop at accountability, you will never see those changes manifest. You must have action along with it, you must be responsible to yourself, your teammates, peers, coaches, parents etc. Responsibility is the action to recognize the mistake, acknowledge your part in it and make the changes or adjustments necessary to not experience that result again! It is easy to be accountable, it is much harder to be responsible, responsibility comes with a price to be paid, with action, with work, with focus and with time. Are you accountable or responsible?

Talent vs. Skill:

Talent refers to a natural ability or gift that some people are born with. Talents make certain activities feel or appear easy, but even the most talented people need practice to truly master the ability. Talent is like having a head start in a race, but it won't guarantee success unless you keep running.

Skill, on the other hand, is acquired and honed over time through practice, discipline, and persistence. A person can become highly proficient through hard work, strategic learning and practice. In fact, the psychology "10,00-hour rule" suggests that mastery often comes from sustained effort rather than natural ability.

The real magic happens when talent meets skill: those who combine their innate strengths with focused practice excel in ways that seem effortless. Talent and skill can work together. If you're talented at something and work hard to develop your skills, you can reach even greater heights. Success isn't just for the naturally gifted—it's for anyone who's willing to put in the effort!

Activity 14: Action Statement:

Your action statement is a combination of your affirmation statement and your non-negotiables. It is a powerful, positive reinforcement of your commitment and your relentless dedication to achieving that commitment.

I am a powerful, inspiring, relentless man, I will never quit, I will never give up, I will never stop until the "commitment" is complete. I will keep working!

Write your action statement on the top of the back of your commitment card.

<u>Team:</u> As a team, create your action statement. You will read it daily!

Chapter 5: W.I.N

Now that you have learned what it means to W.I.N., it is time to execute. The harder you are willing to work, the more time and effort you are willing to put in and dedicate, the more successful you will be. How the W.I.N. program fits in your life, character, commitments and activities is completely up to you. Implementation and execution of the techniques, ideas practices, and processes can be difficult at times, but continued effort will create the habits necessary for success. Here are a couple of thoughts, suggestions, and ideas to help you incorporate W.I.N. into your life.

ATTITUDE

"Virtually nothing is impossible in this world if you just put your mind to it and maintain a positive attitude." – Lou Holtz

Talent is a gift not a promise. Just because you have been given a certain amount of talent doesn't promise success. Attitude is the key to success. Your attitude influences your thoughts, actions, effort, and ultimately determines the outcomes you achieve. A positive attitude directly affects your mindset, turning challenges into opportunities for growth rather than obstacles. This resilience is crucial, especially in sports, where setbacks and challenges are inevitable. Athletes with a strong attitude bounce back from failures, maintain optimism, and consistently push toward their goals. In life, the same attitude helps you navigate personal and professional setbacks with grace, empowering you to persist through difficulties and seize opportunities.

Your attitude impacts those around you, enhancing relationships and creating supportive environments. While talent, skills, and hard work are all essential, it is your attitude that determines how far you will go in sports and life, by cultivating a positive, resilient attitude, you set yourself up for success, no matter what challenges come your way.

Kurt Warner, the hall of fame QB of the super bowl winning St Louis Rams, was stocking shelves at night in a local grocery store while he was training and working towards his commitment of playing in the NFL. He decided that he would make his isle the best isle in the entire store, he took pride in his isle being clean, organized, and all the labels faced out and were in the correct alignment in the shelves. Did stocking shelves at night help him become a better QB? Not athletically, but mentally, he found a positive spin to the mundane task of stocking shelves by focusing on and taking pride in the littlest of tasks and doing them to the absolute best of his ability. He determined that having a positive attitude and focusing on the way stocking shelves could influence, improve, and affect his goal of playing in the NFL would transfer over to his training and performance as a football player. He was right!

CHANGING YOUR ATTTITUDE WILL CHANGE YOUR RESULT!

Hint: Maintaining a positive attitude in the face of tragedy, trials, challenges and loss is one of the most difficult things in life. Having faith in the journey and maintaining a positive mindset that all things contribute to our learning, growing and ultimately our success is powerful tool against the negative thoughts, feelings, and influences around you. Having faith in a higher purpose and a higher power is a great way to control and direct your thoughts and actions in times of struggle.

BREATH IS LIFE

The first and last thing your body does is take a breath. Learning how and why your body uses breathing to benefit, heal, and protect itself is important. Your body increases its respiratory rate to meet higher oxygen demands and remove excess carbon dioxide during physical activity, stress, and metabolic changes. This adjustment ensures adequate oxygen delivery to muscles and organs, maintains pH balance, and responds to environmental conditions. By dynamically adjusting the respiratory rate, the body maintains homeostasis and optimal function under various internal and external conditions.

One of the strongest indicators of stress is your respiratory rate and breathing pattern. An elevated respiratory rate can lead to hyperventilation, inefficient oxygen use, increased fatigue, heightened stress and anxiety, and cardiovascular strain. Learning to regulate breathing is crucial for stress management during sports as it ensures optimized oxygen delivery, enhances endurance, promotes relaxation, maintains mental clarity, and supports consistent performance.

Controlled breathing techniques activate the parasympathetic nervous system, aiding in recovery and preventing fatigue, thereby significantly improving overall performance and well-being. Physically, they improve oxygenation, lung function, heart health, and pain management. Mentally, they reduce stress, enhance focus, and improve sleep quality. Emotionally, they help manage anxiety, regulate mood, and increase emotional resilience.

The US military employs the box breathing technique for its service men and women, and it is my preferred method as well. Box breathing has been proven to:

- **Improve mental well-being:** Breathing is inextricably linked to cognitive activity such as thinking and reasoning. According to studies, taking slow, mindful breaths helps reduce stress and feelings of depression.
- **Heighten cognitive performance:** Box breathing clears the mind, allowing for greater focus and concentration. Taking slow, controlled breaths helps balance our nervous system, which allows us to clear our

minds and increase our attentiveness.

- **Enhance the body's future reactions to stress:** Researchers discovered that regular deep breathing exercises can activate the genes associated with your body's energy and insulin levels while decreasing those associated with inflammation and stress.

- **Help deactivate the fight-or-flight response:** When the sympathetic nervous system is activated, the body goes into "fight, flight, or freeze" mode, preparing itself to "fight" for survival by releasing cortisol. A panic attack occurs when the body enters this mode without being triggered. Deep breathing causes the body to enter the parasympathetic or "rest and digest" mode, which helps calm it down in stressful situations.

Overall, controlled breathing strengthens the mind-body connection, boosts immunity, and enhances athletic and mental performance. Breathing techniques should be practiced regularly to reap these benefits and improve overall quality of your life. There are dozens of different breathing exercises and techniques, I suggest you try several and decide what works best for you. *Hint: Combining Meta-Com principals with your breathing exercises, practices and routines is like a natural performance, focus, and confidence enhancing drug. The effects of breathing on your mental, physical, and emotional state are proven when you add Meta-Com communication to it the results are exponential.*

Activity 15: Box Breathing

1 -Close your eyes. Gradually take a full inhalation through the nose while counting one, two, three, four. With each count draw in more air, so when you reach the count of four, you inhale to your maximum.

2- Hold your breath as you count one, two, three, four again.

3- Then slowly exhale through the mouth, again counting from one to four.

4- After full exhalation, hold your breath again for a count of four.

5- Repeat this cycle at least 4 times. It is recommended to repeat for 5 minutes when possible. I encourage you to add this exercise to your morning and evening routine. Incorporating breathing into your daily affirmations creates a habitual response in your body of calming, positive energy.

**Adding your affirmation statements to your breathing routine is another way to take it up a notch. When you inhale and again when you exhale, repeat your affirmation statement in your mind. You can use multiple statements for each cycle or repeat the same one several times.*

***There are lots of different breathing techniques and exercises. I highly encourage you to find one that works for you and incorporate it into your daily life. This method is often referred to as box breathing; it is widely used by the military and law enforcement.*

<u>*Team:*</u> *As a team, follow the steps above. I recommend you incorporate breathing exercises into your daily training routine(s).*

ROUTINE = HABIT = CHARACTER = WIN

Routines form habits, which in turn shape character, ultimately leading to success. Success is built from the ground up, beginning with routines (consistent, intentional actions that guide you toward your commitments). Over time, these routines become habits, automatic behaviors that free up mental energy, create efficiency, and lead to progress. Habits shape your character. Leading to achieving your goals, realizing your potential, and aligning your actions with your fundamental values (W's).

Pre-Performance Routines (PPRs) are a great way to create positive, uplifting, and focused habits of success. PPR's are structured sequences of actions completed before performing a task or event to enhance mental and physical focus and readiness. For example, in sports like basketball, top free-throw shooters often use a PPR to refocus and relax before each shot. PPRs should be tailored to individual needs and preferences, incorporating activities like visualization, deep breathing, and relaxation exercises to reduce anxiety and build confidence. These habits allow you to perform efficiently, reducing distractions and maximizing focus.

Your PPR should incorporate elements, words, or phrases from your I Am statement(s). It should also include Meta-Com practices and keys to focus your intentions, calm your thoughts, and check your emotions.

- Wake up every morning and do this (set the table):
- Before a performance (prepare and focus)
- During the performance (remind, refocus)
- During a challenge do this (redirect, refocus)
- After performance (sharpen the saw)
- Daily before bed (clean the slate)

Hint: It is effective to include a physical action or signal with your PPR routine. They serve as a quick, powerful, external reminder of your commitment, motivation, and purpose.

Personal PPR are a great way to remember your W's, focus your thoughts and emotions, gain control and confidence and allow yourself to perform your best in that moment. They are also the foundation for building effective, structured, and powerful habits in your life. Routines become habits, and your habits define your character, and your character defines your success.

Activity 16: Creating Positive Habits

1. *Start Small: Identify one small routine you can implement today. It could be as simple as drinking a glass of water every morning.*
2. *Stay Consistent: Commit to repeating this routine daily. Consistency is key in the transition from routine to habit.*
3. *Reflect and Adjust: Regularly reflect on your habits. Are they helping you become the person (player) you want to be? Make adjustments as needed.*
4. *Focus on Character Development: Think about the traits you want to embody. Align your habits with these traits.*
5. *Celebrate Small Wins: Every step forward, no matter how small, is progress. Celebrate these wins to keep motivation high.*

<u>Team:</u> As a team, follow the steps above, small changes will produce big results as you change negative habits, thoughts, actions and practices within your team culture you will experience big rewards.

T.E.A.M. (Together Everyone Achieves More)

"We are stronger together than we are alone" -Walter Payton

W.I.N. is as much about your team as is it about yourself. No one accomplishes greatness by themselves. Your W's are about you, but you can and should have W's for your team, employees, family, peer group, etc. Establishing W's as a group allows each member to clearly identify their role, responsibility, and contribution to the team commitments. Whether you are the boss, the experienced contributor or the newbie you have and play an important role for your team to W.I.N.

Collaboration leads to greater success than individual efforts. By working together, each member contributes their unique skills and resources, leading to enhanced outcomes and the ability to achieve shared goals and commitments. The concept emphasizes that unity and mutual support within a team result in more significant accomplishments and effectiveness than working alone.

The importance of a team in your success lies in the collaborative support, diverse skills, and shared goals that a team provides. Being part of a team allows you to leverage collective knowledge and expertise, which can enhance problem-solving, and innovation. Teams offer encouragement, motivation, and constructive feedback, helping individuals overcome challenges and improve their performance. Additionally, teamwork fosters a sense of accountability and shared responsibility, which can drive individuals to perform at their best. Ultimately, the synergy of a well-functioning team can amplify an individual's strengths, compensate for weaknesses, and contribute significantly to achieving personal and collective success; it is called the Pygmalion effect.

The Pygmalion effect is a psychological phenomenon where higher standard and expectations placed on individuals lead to improved performance and outcomes. This effect occurs when a person's performance is influenced positively by the expectations others have of them. For example, if a teacher believes a student is capable of high achievement, the student is more likely to excel due to the increased support, encouragement, and positive feedback they receive. The Pygmalion effect highlights the powerful impact of belief and expectations on individual potential, demonstrating that positive reinforcement and faith in someone's abilities can significantly enhance their success.

When team leaders and members hold a high standard for each other, it fosters a supportive environment where individuals are motivated to meet and exceed those expectations. This positive reinforcement leads to increased confidence, effort, and collaboration, ultimately improving team outcomes.

Teams are important because they bring together diverse skills, perspectives, and strengths, which enhance problem-solving and innovation. They provide a support network that helps individuals overcome challenges, stay motivated, and achieve collective goals. The synergy within a well-functioning team, combined with high expectations, amplifies individual contributions and drives the team toward greater success.

Surround yourself with others that share your character, determination, commitments and who will hold you to a higher standard. Great teammates are not the ones who tell you how great you are all the time; they are the ones who see your greatness and push you towards it. Be a great teammate, surround yourself with great teammates, and W.I.N. together.

Hint: Share your commitments cards with others you can trust, that want to see you succeed. It is a great way to add another level of accountability and great teammates will hold you accountable to the standard and commitments you have set for yourself.

TRENDING

"I lost a lot of games in my career, but I never became a loser,"
- Aeneas Williams.

You will lose in your life; in fact, most people will lose more than they win over the course of their lives, not just in the athletic arena but in their life, their careers, etc. What will remain with you is yourself. Losing builds character, creates humility, and gives you a view into the soul of a person. It provides insight into what you need to do and what you have accomplished on your way through failure. It is easy to handle winning. It is much more difficult to handle losing. The difference between winning and losing (success and failure) is what you focus on. The way to never lose is to always compete against yourself. Compete against your previous self, compete against your natural tendency to make excuses, slack off, be lazy, or even quit. Compete against your goals and your personal bests! Compete, compete, compete! Fight for what you want and do your best! Learn from challenges, learn from defeat, but never allow yourself to become a loser!

Every challenge is an opportunity to learn, improve and test yourself. Winning is not about avoiding challenges; it's about the process, the development, and the improvement that occurs along the way.

A great way to maintain a positive perception of challenges is to look at your trajectory, not your position. Ask yourself how am I trending?

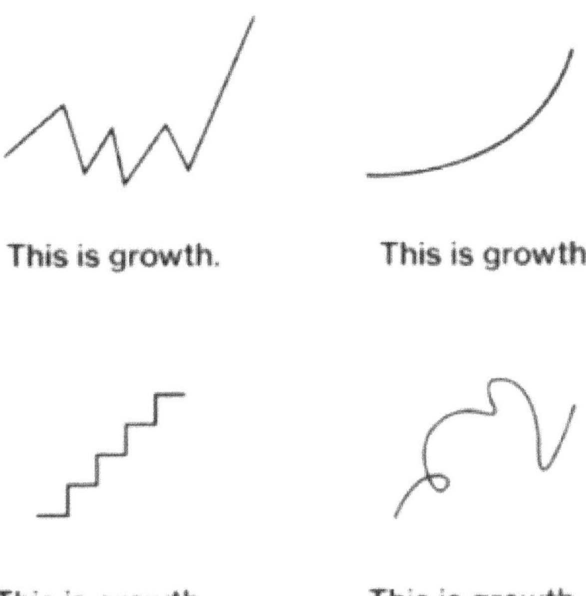

A key to staying motivated and keeping working is to focus on the trajectory, not the position. Did I accomplish my ultimate goal? Did I get closer to it today? I am on an upward, or forward trajectory? Focusing on the direction you are headed programs your mind to never be satisfied, never quit or give up, and to keep working. Focusing on the trajectory and not the achievement gives you the motivation you need to keep going. I got closer today, and I am still trending upward toward reaching my goal. The only was to lose is to give up and quit. If you are still working, still trying and still moving you are still growing and improving, you are still winning!

W.I.N.

"The answers to these questions will determine your success or failure. 1.) Can people trust me to do what's right? 2.) Am I committed to doing my best? 3.) Do I care about other people and show it? If the answers to these questions are yes, there is no way you can fail." -Lou Holtz

Ultimately winning is determined, measured and achieved differently for us all. Just like fingerprints, none of us have the same W's (goals, dreams, commitments, and motivations) Winning for one may be to make the team, for another it is to start and play varsity, a smaller group likely won't consider it a win without playing in college or even the professional level, and yet there is still the few who won't stop until they are the greatest of all time. Winning is measured against your individual commitments and the sacrifices you are willing to make to W.I.N. Success is achieved along the journey to fulfilling those commitments. Regardless of your personal definition, standard, and commitment; there is always a way to win.

Over the years my definition, of winning has changed dramatically, and so will yours. In my youth, I set commitments to achieve certain goals centered around athletics, and as I advanced in life, those commitments changed to a career and lifestyle focus for myself and my family. I am at a point in my life now where being a great father and husband to successful, happy, and high character children is my definition of W.I.N. I love being a father, and I love being a coach, assisting my kids, athletes and clients to define, and achieve their own W.I.N.s.

W.I.N. is about you; it is about who you are, and who and what you want to become. What your goals and commitments are and what you are willing to do to make those a reality. It takes effort, it takes practice, it takes falling and getting back up, but it does work. Trust the process and trust yourself. You will W.I.N.

Learning to use the principles in this book you will create a winner. You are a winner, you can and will win. It is easy to pick up this book, read or watch something online that motivates you, inspires you and even teaches you, but in order for it to mean anything, to have any value at all you have to implement, practice, work for it and use it.

Chapter 6: FINAL THOUGHTS

I like to leave every training session, seminar or speaking engagement with a with an idea, principle, thought or quote to think about. I have learned that sometimes the greatest lessons come from the simplest thought-provoking comments, concepts, and ideas.

LEADERSHIP

"Leadership is not about being in charge. It's about taking care of those in your charge." -Mike Tomlin

Leadership's not about wielding authority or being at the top, but about the responsibility to support, nurture, and guide those you lead. A great leader understands that their role isn't just to lead their team but to serve them, providing the resources, encouragement, and environment needed for individuals to thrive and succeed. There are two distinct types of leadership:

The Commanding Leader: This type of leader leads from the front, setting the pace and expecting others to keep up. They are often focused on results and personal achievement, driving the team forward with clear direction and high expectations. While they can be effective in reaching goals, their primary motivation is often centered around receiving credit, recognition, and being seen as the primary force behind the team's success. They ensure that the team follows, but they make it clear that they're in charge and often seek the spotlight.

The Servant Leader: This leader takes a more flexible approach, shifting between roles as needed. Sometimes they lead from the front, inspiring and guiding; other times, they push from behind, encouraging and supporting; and often, they work from within the group, observing, learning, and empowering others. Their focus is on the team's overall success and the personal growth of each member, rather than their own accolades. This leader prioritizes the well-being and development of the team, ensuring everyone has the opportunity to achieve their best.

Taking care of those in your charge, you foster trust, loyalty, and a shared commitment to collective goals. Ultimately, leadership is about creating a space where everyone feels valued, empowered, and equipped to contribute their best, knowing that their leader has their back every step of the way. You do NOT have to be the best to be a leader! The best coaches were often not the best players. The best leaders are often not the best player. Leadership is love, services, dedication and honesty.

Leadership should be deeply rooted in your "why" (your purpose and commitment to serving something greater than yourself.) If you are "trying" to lead in a direction that isn't in alignment with your why, then you are wasting your time and the time of the people you are "trying" to lead. True leadership is about serving others and helping them reach their potential rather than seeking personal glory. True leadership isn't about accolades, awards, or being in the spotlight; it's about ensuring that everyone on the team is empowered to achieve their own personal best on the path to a collective victory. By focusing on serving others and fostering an environment where everyone can thrive, you embody the essence of authentic leadership.

Great leadership is the true manifestation of success in my book. There are those that make it to the top seemingly in their own. The truth is those people are either ungrateful, selfish, or liars. No one accomplished anything alone! Leaders are grateful for those individuals that have helped them; even the smallest act of kindness or opportunity to learn, teach or lead can make a huge impact on your life and the lives of those you have the opportunity to come in contact with. Reaching the top and bringing others with you or reaching back down to help those who are stumbling on their way up is the real victory in life. Happiness comes from service, and the greatest form of service is leading and guiding other to achieve their best! BE A LEADER!

WINNERS WANT IT MORE:

"Never die easy. Why run out of bounds and die easy? Make that linebacker pay. It carries into all facets of your life. It's okay to lose, to die, but don't die without trying, without giving it your best." -Walter Payton

Walter Payton is widely regarded as the best all-around football player of all time. He was not the biggest or the fastest. The majority of his career his offensive line was average at best. He was extremely talented, but he was never the most naturally skilled athlete. The reason he is the best came down to one thing.... He wanted it more. He trained harder than anyone else, he outworked everyone, he never quit, he never gave up. His famous quote of "Never die easy" wasn't just in relation to his terminal illness, he meant it for every single play he played, he lived it with every single breath he took. He simply wanted it more. He had a relentless will to win, every moment of everyday and in every way.

We all want to be winners; we all want to be successful. The question is not if you want to win. The question is if you are willing to do what it takes to win; do you have the will to win? Everyone want to be a champion until it comes time to do what champions do. It is hard, it is challenging, it requires sacrifice, blood sweat and tears. Success is earned by those who want it the most; by those who are willing to do what it takes to achieve it.

YOU ARE A WINNER

"Be a pro. • Act like a champion. • Respond to adversity; don't react. • Be on time. Being late means either it's not important to you or you can't be relied upon. • Execute. Do what you're supposed to do when you're supposed to do it. Not almost. All the way. Not most of the time. All of the time. • Take ownership. Whatever it takes. No excuses, no explanations." - Tony Dungy

Winning is not an occasional occurrence or momentary achievement, that you just stumble into. To be a winner, you must develop winning habits, traits, practices, routines, and commitments. You can win the battle but lose the war. Your W.I.N. journey is the same, you can do a few of the practices, and fake a couple more, maybe half-ass one or two and ride the coattails of others to a few victories but to truly win, YOU must become a winner. Focus on your fundamentals, control your controllables and pursue your commitments with unrelenting passion and effort. Be better today than you were yesterday and make tomorrow better than today. Consistent, dedicated, focused effort on improving yourself is the secret to wining every day! If you improved today, then you won today, if you learned today then you won today and if you gave your best today, then you won today. You are here to make a difference, to affect others in a positive way. We are all members of the same team, and the more we do to help each other, the higher we will all reach.

You are a winner, you can and will win. Be accountable, coachable, and relentless in the pursuit of of your commitments (winning); serve others, and always do your best! When you do that you cannot lose! You are a winner!

Appendix

Commitment Cards: *Free Printable PDF or Digital Version available on our website: www.clutchmentality.com*

Commitment cards are a great reminder of your personal commitment and contract with yourself for achievement. They are most effective when they are placed in a location that you will see and read them often. You can even carry them with you and review them throughout your day.

I also encourage you to share them with your circle of influence, those individuals who want to see you succeed and will hold you accountable to your commitments.

Team: I recommend that you have several posters made of your team commitment card(s). Place them in the locker room, in the film room, weight room, etc. You want your team to see these multiple times per day.

You can also send them out daily in text messages, pictures etc.

-Repeat your team gratitude statement, and/or affirmation statement daily as a team. The more your team buys into these commitments, the less time you will spend on managing bad or lazy behavior, grades, attendance, etc.

Sample Commitment Card:

Suggestions for Coaches and Teams:

I encourage you to use W.I.N. as an annual manual and team activity that you engage in throughout the year. The activities can be completed as a team, small group, and individually. Creating a process and program that you incorporate into your training both during the season and in the off-season emphasizes the culture you want year-round. True culture change is changing the habits your team has from the top to the bottom. Team and team members commitments are just as important during the off-season as they are during the season. Coaching is not a seasonal gig; it is a lifelong commitment to the improvement of your team individually and collectively. Here are a few suggestions that I have found to be very effective in changing habits, installing accountability and increasing success.

<u>Small Groups</u>: Depending on the size of your team, divide them into groups of 6 or less. Use senior members of the team as group captains.

- You can assign these teams or do a draft method where group captains take turn choosing their team members.
- Captains are responsible to lead, motivate, communicate, include and friendship their team members.
- Captains are the communication between their team and the coaching staff. This includes missing or being late for practice, training, or team functions, concerns for personal issues, grades, girlfriend or boyfriend, family matters, etc.
- Each member of your staff is assigned a group or groups to oversee and be responsible for.
- Creating small groups increases participation, accountability and team unity. Teams start to encourage, support and police each other in their groups and on the team, especially when you incorporate a points program and awards.

Points Program:

- Rewarding good behavior is more powerful than punishing bad behavior, especially in teens.
- Create or use a program that allows you to reward attendance, grades,

participation, effort, great plays, service or any other positive actions with points.

- Awarding the top points earner and group at the end of the year with some great prizes will shift your culture and accountability from you and your staff to the group captains, team leaders and individual social group leaders.

Commitment Cards:

- Encourage each member of your team to share their individual commitment cards with their groups and with a member of the staff (position coach, group assigned coach, etc).
- Sharing commitment cards is a great way to keep members motivated and on track. This is also a great way to remind members what their goals were when they started.
- Review of commitment cards with group captains and a coach throughout the year are a simple and effective way to get a feel for the culture and direction of the team on an individual level throughout the season.

www.ingramcontent.com/pod-product-compliance
Lightning Source LLC
Chambersburg PA
CBHW051133160726
47997CB00019B/2373